WESLEYAN THEOLOGICAL PERSPECTIVES

TREASURE THE WORD

WESLEYAN THEOLOGICAL PERSPECTIVES

TREASURE THE WORD

*A Layperson's Guide
to Interpreting Scripture*

Edited by Joseph Coleson

wesleyan
publishing
house

Indianapolis, Indiana

Copyright © 2009 by Wesleyan Publishing House
Published by Wesleyan Publishing House
Indianapolis, Indiana 46250
Printed in the United States of America
ISBN: 978-0-89827-412-7

To the memory of saints both ancient and modern
who died because they dared to translate the Scriptures,
and with deepest gratitude and affection for those who have
been our guides to the priceless treasure of their pages.

CONTENTS

FOREWORD

I n this century, many of us are appalled that people in the eighteenth and early nineteenth centuries based their justification of slavery on Scripture. But as people began to read the Scriptures more holistically in the Wesleys' time, debates began. Eyes were opened, and abolitionism was born. It became a bitter battle, first in England and then on through our Civil War here in the United States. Ultimately, the Wesleyan Methodist Church was formed amid this turmoil. From our earliest existence, we were firmly grounded on what has become known more recently as the "Wesleyan Quadrilateral" as our guide for biblical interpretation:

- Scripture—The Holy Bible, including both the Old and New Testaments
- Tradition—The two-millennia-long history of the Christian church
- Reason—Rational thinking and sensible interpretation
- Experience—Christians' personal and communal journeys with Christ

In one of my readings on the history of South Africa, I found again how the interpretation of the Old Testament in particular had convinced the settlers from Europe of their special authority over the indigenous peoples of the region. They saw themselves as God's chosen people for South Africa. This reading justified their conquering its land and peoples in the same manner as Joshua conquered Canaan. This injustice

9

and misreading of Scripture lasted for centuries, resulting in the system called Apartheid, which was dismantled late in the twentieth century.

This is only one modern example of the various misinterpretations of Scripture that have marginalized people from the body of Christ due to race, class, or gender. The looming question becomes, How do we read Scripture for it to be truly "bread of life," as God intended?

This volume can become a companion to your Bible in that quest. Reading Scripture first through the eyes of the cultures in and to which it was written is always interesting. But, just as important, it's also immensely instructive for our understanding. Your cultural and historical eyes will be opened in this volume.

Another crucial aspect of our reading is the various uses of language: metaphors and other figurative language, analogies, allegories, parables, and more. This is where misinterpretation often happens, as truth becomes lost in misunderstanding. This volume will help the reader learn to find the treasures of truth embedded in the biblical authors' use of language on all its levels.

One of the treasures of Scripture is its coherence. Put another way, the grand themes of Scripture run coherently throughout, from beginning to end. We can—we must—interpret the text by keeping the whole in mind, and often by using other texts for the illumination of those which are difficult or obscure.

But even more helpful than the technical aspects of this volume is the spirit of the authors. Their goal is to bring you, the reader, into greater conformity with the character of Christ as you embrace Scripture and allow the Holy Spirit to assist in the interpretive process.

I am delighted with the previous volumes in this series: *Passion, Power, and Purpose* (on preaching); *The Church Jesus Builds*; and *Be Holy*. I'm confident this volume will find a valued place among them. Thanks to the many authors and the vision of editor Joseph

Coleson for placing Wesleyan thought as a firm foundation for our action in the twenty-first century.

Today we are surrounded by economic uncertainty, wars, HIV/AIDS, modern-day slavery, abortion, and secularism. It seems that each day brings a new crisis. People are rushing hither and yon for hope and answers. It's a sign of hope that many are turning to the Scriptures.

Recently, a *Washington Times* reporter traveling to Africa with President George W. Bush phoned me for my thoughts on aid to Africa. At the end of our conversation he asked, in rather desperate tones, "Jo Anne, why do you do what you do?" I found my immediate response somewhat surprising myself, as I began my answer straight from the words of Jesus: "Jesus said in one of his final prayers, '*As* the Father has sent me I am now sending you.' The word *as* means doing what Jesus has done." He didn't respond on the other end, but I kept going. "But then Jesus said something even more compelling; he said we would do even greater things than he has done, because he was going to the Father."

Now I was afraid I had totally lost this reporter, but I was too far into this one-way discussion to stop, so I continued. "Jesus' going to the Father means he has sent his Holy Spirit to us, his power and wisdom living within us; therefore, we will be able to do what he has done in various ways." There was intense silence on the other end, and I thought he had hung up. I was ready to ask the familiar "Can you hear me now?" question, when a faint voice on the other end said, "Wow! Will you please pray for me on my trip to Africa?"

I have reflected many times on this conversation. Somehow, the power of Scripture spoke deeply into the heart of this reporter. I believe through this volume we will renew our vision of God's redemptive plan and purpose in the universe and our place as his people in this plan.

It's my prayer that we will restore our courage in God's presence and Word to move into some of the most difficult and dark places of this world to bring his healing and hope. God is calling us today. But he's also giving us the tools.

—Jo Anne Lyon
General Superintendent
The Wesleyan Church

ACKNOWLEDGMENTS

W*esleyan Theological Perspectives* is made possible through the support of the Wesleyan Education Council, comprising the presidents and deans of four liberal arts universities—Houghton College, Indiana Wesleyan University, Oklahoma Wesleyan University, and Southern Wesleyan University—and of Bethany Bible College. These are the educational institutions sponsored by the North American General Conference of The Wesleyan Church. We are grateful for their continued generous support of this and other projects of our steering committee, comprising the university chairs in religion, the dean of the Bible college, and the series editor.

This fourth volume in the series was planned and shaped by Kelvin Friebel (Houghton), Kenneth Gavel (Bethany), Kerry Kind (TWC), Steve Lennox (IWU), Roger McKenzie (SWU), Mark Weeter (OWU), Joseph Coleson (NTS, chair), and Charlotte Coleson (assisting as recording secretary, in a focused set of meetings in February 2008, in Indianapolis, Ind.). We thank all of them for their invaluable contributions.

Kerry Kind, General Director of the Department of Education and the Ministry, The Wesleyan Church, and Don Cady, General Publisher, Wesleyan Publishing House, have been unfailingly supportive of this project, and wise in their counsel from the beginning. Kevin Scott, editor, Wesleyan Publishing House, provided significant in-house editorial support.

The Board of General Superintendents has given its enthusiastic endorsement of this project from its inception; we thank all its members, past and present. They have led the way in the acceptance and use of these volumes across our beloved church.

You, our esteemed reader, have our heartfelt thanks, also. Putting these volumes on your study shelf has given our efforts a place. Taking them off your shelf and reading them gives us reason to hope we have not undertaken this work in vain. *Gloria in excelsis Deo.*

INTRODUCTION

THE ART AND SCIENCE OF BIBLE INTERPRETATION

Joseph Coleson

Treasure! The very word conjures images of lost gold mines, sunken ships, or safe deposit boxes filled with loose diamonds, pearl necklaces, and emerald pendants. In this book, we are using *treasure* as a metaphor for biblical study for two reasons. First, the Bible, and the kingdom of God to which it points us, are treasures vastly beyond the worth of anything we could possess, or even imagine, on this earthly plane. Second, as with most physical treasure, acquiring the real treasures hidden in the Bible requires effort on our part. It's not that God desires to keep the treasure hidden from us. Rather, we need to learn the ways to the treasure-house, learn to use the keys that unlock it, and learn to know and use the treasures once we are inside.

THAT SEMI-SCARY WORD, "HER-MEH-*NEW*-TICS"

For some years I team-taught an introductory course in biblical hermeneutics; we defined it as "the art and science of interpretation." That definition is still good and, technically, this is a volume on several important aspects of biblical hermeneutics.

But I don't want that to scare you, or cause you to put this book down, saying, "It's not for me." In less technical terms, this is a book of down-to-earth information and advice we all need to get the most value, inspiration and, yes, enjoyment from our reading and study of that most important book for every Christian, the Bible. All the contributors to this volume have discovered that intensive study, as well as more casual reading of the Bible, is both a great joy and a source of strength, instruction, wisdom, and comfort in our Christian walk and in our ministry assignments. We hope these pages will help you in the same ways we've been helped.

We all interpret. We interpret when we listen. You know the difference between sincere agreement and sarcastic or even angry disagreement just by the tone of voice of the one speaking to you. If you're in the presence of the one with whom you're speaking, your mind interprets both what you hear and what you see. What you see is often called body language, and it can be very important to correct interpretation.

We also interpret when we read. In fact, it's impossible to read without interpreting. You may have heard (though I hope not!) some preacher or teacher say, "Don't interpret the Bible; just read it and apply it." The attempt to do so is often very damaging, both to the one reading, and to everyone he or she attempts to teach using that approach.

Reading is a form of listening, because writing is a form of speech. If anything, care in interpreting is more important when we read than when we listen, because we are usually not in the presence of the writer. The author cannot say, "Oh, I didn't mean that; I meant this." We must learn to pick up on the written clues, because we can't read the writer's visual and oral clues, nor the tone of voice and the body language. But the written word does come with its own abundance of clues and cues. We just have to learn how to read them, and that is what this book is about. We hope to help you become better at reading and understanding what you read in the Bible as you gain a better understanding of, and more developed skills in, reading the Bible in the various ways its human authors present it to us.

The Bible is both a divine and a human book. Every contributor to this volume affirms that God is the divine initiating author; that's why the Bible is the most important book ever written. But we also know God invited many human authors to partner in the writing of its varied parts. God's invitation to participate in this synergistic project did not require the human authors to suppress their personalities, their educational backgrounds, or their life experiences. Rather, God allowed and encouraged them to express all these, and a great many more aspects of their beings. The Bible is divine revelation expressed in human language, spoken in and to human cultures, times, and circumstances. It truly is a divine/human partnership, written at God's initiative and by virtue of human response.

If I say more along these lines, I'll be stealing my colleagues' thunder, so let me give you a brief orientation to our volume, and a hint or two of how to get the most from it.

FINDING YOUR WAY AROUND THE BOOK

Part 1: A Wesleyan Context for Interpreting Scripture is a kind of overview of biblical interpretation and understanding from a Wesleyan point of view. Chapter 1 sets the tone, reminding us of the many ways the Bible is important to the Christian believer, both personally and in community. You will find this chapter inspirational and informative, (re)awakening your desire to unlock and enter the treasure house the Bible truly is.

Wesleyans count John and Charles Wesley as important spiritual forebears. Chapter 2 orients us to John Wesley's high view of Scripture, his reasons for holding that high view, and some of the important principles he used to arrive at his interpretations. Chapter 3 presents the three principles which, along with the high view of Scripture as the Christian's first authority, are often referred to as the "Wesleyan Quadrilateral." Reason, tradition, and experience are not equal with Scripture, but they are important resources in the proper interpretation of Scripture, especially its more obscure or difficult passages or concepts.

Chapter 4 takes the history of Wesleyan biblical interpretation beyond Wesley, sketching the major currents influencing Wesleyan/Holiness interpretive thinking and methods down to the present. It then suggests several issues we need to attend to, if we would continue to be Wesleyan in our views and handling of Scripture in and for the twenty-first century.

Taken together, these first four chapters are a brief history of, and orientation to, Wesleyan biblical interpretation. The reader who desires to know and be immersed in the Wesleyan interpretive ethos will find them invaluable.

Part 2: A Tool Kit for Interpreting Scripture comprises six chapters introducing several of the most important elements of the careful study of Scripture, if we want to understand and teach it correctly. They are not a how-to or a step-by-step manual, but these chapters will enlarge your understanding of what to look for when studying the Bible, and apprentice you in the use of new skills.

The first three chapters of the section deal with genre, culture, and figurative language, orienting the reader to three essential factors present in every biblical text. The student of the Bible who learns to recognize them and interpret them accordingly is on the way to understanding what God and the human authors intended us to read. The one who ignores or misreads them will go wrong in some way, large or small, every time; it's inevitable. These chapters will reward the reader's careful study and his or her investigation of their examples in their biblical contexts.

The subjects of chapters 8, 9, and 10 include the importance of reading theologically, of recognizing the divine/human authorship of the text, and of understanding the progressive nature of God's revelation in the divine pages through more than thirteen hundred years. These issues are lenses through which we must do our interpretation—through which all interpretation is done, consciously or not. We interpret well if we use these lenses consciously, conscientiously, and consistently; we interpret poorly, if we do not. Again, it's inevitable. These chapters will help you interpret well.

Part 3: A Wesleyan Approach to Interpreting Scripture comprises two chapters. Chapter 11 deals with the Bible as language, from word, phrase, clause, and paragraph, to intertextual (across the Bible) interpretation. In a number of ways, this is the capstone of the book. It demonstrates the content of previous chapters, as well as teaching and illustrating the multiplex importance of language at all levels. Though the longest chapter in the book, it will richly reward multiple readings and study.

Chapter 12 is a collection of shorter examples culled from our teaching and preaching and our listening and learning over the years of our ministries. Some are examples we should follow; others point us in the opposite direction. Many examples will illustrate more than one principle or subject presented in previous chapters. We hope each will provide you with an "Ah-ha!" moment.

A final note: you will occasionally notice a brief mention in one chapter of an issue covered more extensively in another. We have minimized these, but some are unavoidable and even desirable. We cannot isolate our various interpretive moves; they work together. Think of these as mutually reinforcing, rather than as unnecessary repetition.

I invite you now to turn the page and approach the door. As you do, I pray that you will experience many rewarding hours in the treasure-house of God's Word.

PART 1

A WESLEYAN CONTEXT FOR INTERPRETING SCRIPTURE

THE TREASURE OF SCRIPTURE

❖

Stephen J. Lennox

*"The word of the Lord stands forever." And this is the
word that was preached to you.*

—1 Peter 1:25

Here is knowledge enough for me. Let me be
homo unius libri [a man of one book].

—John Wesley

Aman of one book" is how John Wesley described himself. He read extensively, wrote many volumes, and actively promoted the reading of many books among his followers. But he wanted to be known as a man devoted to one book, the Bible. "O give me that book! At any price, give me the book of God," he pleaded.

Others have shared Wesley's high regard for Scripture. The translators of the King James Version, in their dedication to their patron, described the Bible as "that inestimable treasure, which excelleth all the riches of the earth." Johann Gutenberg chose it as the first book to be printed on his revolutionary invention. Today, in the post-Christian

West, the Bible remains the most published book ever, with over one hundred million copies sold or given away each year, and with annual Bible sales, just in the United States, ranging between 425 million and 650 million dollars annually.[1]

REASONS TO TREASURE THE BIBLE

We treasure the Bible for many reasons. One important reason is that it stands as the foundation of Western civilization. The West highly values human beings, due largely to the influence of Genesis 1 which describes us as made in God's image. This is why Woodrow Wilson called the Bible "the 'Magna Carta' of the human soul." It clearly asserts we are moral agents responsible to God. "Whenever a man sees this vision," Wilson affirmed, "he stands up a free man."[2] But the Bible also claims that humans have fallen from God's original design and now are essentially self-centered. This understanding of humanity—made in God's image, but now sinful—is enshrined in the United States Constitution with its insistence on human liberty and with safeguards against the abuse of liberty.

The Bible has influenced Western culture in other ways, such as the importance of science and objective thought. The opening chapter of Genesis emphasizes that God created this world to reproduce "after its kind." Why is this important? Because it clarifies that though God created and provides for this universe, God does so as the one who exists separate from his creation. God designed it to operate by observable laws, such as the law of gravity.

To us this is obvious, but to the ancient pagan mind it was unthinkable. They saw the natural world as an extension of the gods. For example, if it rains because the gods are pleased, then we need a priest, not a weatherman. The biblical view, however, encourages the analysis of natural and historical events, and the formulation of conclusions based on the observation of repeated phenomena. Simply said, we treasure Scripture because it provided the foundation for the scientific and rational approaches which have brought much good into our world.

If you wish to discover how influential the Bible is on Western thought, listen carefully to what people write and say. Scriptural allusions abound in our great writers like Shakespeare, Hawthorne, Melville, Steinbeck, and Updike. Public figures commonly employ biblical themes. Think of Abraham Lincoln's second inaugural address or Martin Luther King, Jr.'s "I have a dream" speech. The Bible shows up daily in the newspaper ("The police demonstrated the patience of Job.") and in everyday conversation ("I guess I should turn the other cheek."). Biblical phrases remain a part of our vocabulary.

Beyond its profound historic and literary influence on our culture, we treasure Scripture because it provides honest and satisfying answers to our deepest questions—the questions that keep us awake at night. Humans wonder where everything came from, why we're here, what is wrong with us, how it can be made right, and where are we going. All religions offer answers to these questions; Christianity's answers are found in the Bible and many, even nonbelievers, acknowledge that Scripture's answers ring truest. God called this world into being as something good and placed us here as God's representatives, highly privileged and highly responsible. Something has gone wrong with God's original design, but the blame lies with us, not with him. Yet God has shown mercy and offers restoration through Christ's sacrifice, not only for us but for this universe as well. We treasure Scripture for giving us true answers to tough questions.

More than answers, however, the Bible provides us with *the* answer. St. Augustine described every person as made for a relationship with God, but with hearts that grow restless "until they find their rest in Thee." The Bible alerts us both to the need and the solution, making it clear that God is personal and desires a relationship with his creation. The Bible affirms our instincts that such a relationship is impossible, since God is holy and we aren't. However, anticipating our objection, the Bible describes a God who loves us enough to make his home here, early on in the tabernacle and temple, and then as one of us. We treasure the Bible, for it reveals God's love for us.

The Bible not only tells us about this love, it allows us to experience it. Imagine you've been reading a travel guide describing a country you've always wanted to visit. At the end of the book, you find a note written to you personally by the publisher, directing you on how to pick up your free plane ticket. The Bible is more than just a book about God; it's a message from God, describing how you can enter into a relationship with him. When I was a boy I always imagined myself as a character in whatever story I was reading. Imagine my delight in discovering that in the case of the Bible, I was right!

When we enter this relationship with God and begin to live God's way, we experience true joy. Sin had us going "against the grain," choosing what promised happiness but delivered much less. We were like people trying to run a car on kerosene. Living in relationship with God allows us to understand who we are, how to relate to others, and how to be wise. The Bible describes the way to abundant life, much as an owner's manual tells you how to get the most from your car. As conscientious car owners keep the manual handy, so Christians treasure this book that explains how to have abundant life.

THE BIBLE AS GOD'S WORD

Letters written by famous people end up in museums; simple notes become treasures because someone famous wrote them. We treasure the Bible because we recognize its author as God. Divine origin best explains why the Bible has provided a solid foundation for Western society, how it answers the core questions of humanity at large, and how honest seekers actually meet the author, finding their stories in God's story.

Other reasons invite us to believe the Bible is God's Word and is therefore worth treasuring. We have reliable testimony from other believers, including, in many instances, the authors themselves who claim to speak for God. We have testimony from authors' contemporaries, such as when Daniel treated Jeremiah's prophecy as Scripture (Dan. 9:2), when Peter applied this term to the writings of Paul (2 Pet. 3:16), or when the early Christians collected Jesus' sayings. We have broader statements, as when Paul wrote that "all Scripture is God-breathed" (2 Tim. 3:16). Moreover, we have the testimony of the early church that certain books came from God and others did not. Eventually, such decisions were made official in a process known as "canonization."

Some misunderstand canonization, imagining church leaders seated around a large table piled high with documents, sorting through various writings, rejecting some and approving others based on what they had decided the Bible should say. Recently, people have heard, for example, that books like the gospel of Judas were left out in a conspiratorial squelching of the minority opinion.

Even a brief consideration of the canonization process puts such concerns to rest. Canonization took centuries, with books gaining or losing favor as congregations used them, thereby discovering their true nature. Eventually church leaders affirmed the conclusions already reached by the church in the laboratory of experience: "It was not so much that the Church selected the canon as that the canon selected itself."[3]

Others object that claims to inspiration are just that—claims—and dismiss them on that basis. Certainly, claiming something to be from God doesn't make it so. Mormons claim the Book of Mormon to be inspired, but Christians reject that claim as false. We reject it, however, not because it is only a claim, but because the claim does not hold up to careful scrutiny. The claims of the authors and recipients of the Bible, when given their day in court, *do* stand up to careful scrutiny.

However, the conclusion that the Bible is inspired is ultimately a step of faith. Even the most capable scholar cannot prove inspiration beyond any doubt. It appears this is just what God intended. Had God wanted the divine origin of the Bible to be an undeniable fact, he could have ensured this in a myriad of ways. Instead, God provided enough evidence to make a strong case, then left us to take that final step on faith.

Those who do believe, however, receive the testimony of one further witness: the Holy Spirit, who as one writer describes, makes the believer "perfectly assured of the Divine origin of truths already accredited as inspired."[4] Well do I remember the settling power of this supernatural testimony as a young graduate student, struggling with challenges to the Bible's authority. What a difference it made as I approached these challenges, taking them with full seriousness, then realizing that the question of the Bible's divine origin was already settled in a higher court. What had been a treasured book now became even more valuable to me.

HOW TO TREASURE THE BIBLE

Throughout the centuries those who treasured the Bible took great pains to protect and preserve it. Copies were produced by hand until the invention of the printing press. This copying was usually done very carefully. One group of copyists, known as the Masoretes, calculated the middle verse, word, and letter of each book to prevent copying errors.[5] Manuscripts were treated with the greatest care and respect and, in times of danger, were hidden or spirited away. Manuscripts too worn for daily use were retired to secure locations. Scholars are not sure whether the Dead Sea Scrolls—manuscripts hidden in caves in the first century A.D. by the community of Jewish "monks" at Qumran—were placed there in retirement, or to protect them from the Romans.

As Christianity spread into new territories, it became necessary to translate the Bible into other languages, work done at great peril to the translator. Many were killed for their efforts, like William Tyndale. Though we are deeply saddened by one group of Christians killing another, the motive behind both the execution of translations and the execution of translators was the high esteem of Scripture. Church officials opposed new translations in order to protect the Bible from abuse by untrained readers. Tyndale and others risked their lives because they wanted people to be able to read the Bible in their own tongues. A reason for thankfulness is that opposition to new translations has all but disappeared, and the passion for translation characteristic of Christianity has produced at least some parts of the Bible in over twenty-three hundred languages.[6]

We who treasure the Bible must do our part to make it available to others, supporting the distribution of Scripture through organizations like the Gideons and the production of translations by groups like Wycliffe Bible Translators. We should also support the continuing production of new translations in English. One of those responsible for the New Living Translation contends that new translations need to be produced in every generation,[7] a view that would have been whole-heartedly supported by the translators of the King James Version. In their notes to the reader, they asserted that ongoing translation work is necessary:

Translation it is that openeth the window, to let in the light; that breaketh the shell, that we may eat the kernel; that putteth aside the curtain, that we may look into the most holy place; that removeth the cover of the well, that we may come by the water . . . Indeed, without translation into the vulgar tongue, the unlearned are but like children at Jacob's well (which was deep) without a bucket or something to draw with: or as that person mentioned by

Isaiah, to whom when a sealed book was delivered, with this motion, "Read this, I pray thee," he was fain to make this answer, "I cannot, for it is sealed."[8]

We must not treasure the Bible for its own sake; that would be idolatry. You can treasure an antique toy by keeping it on the shelf in its original packaging. This does preserve its value, but a shelved toy is something of a paradox. So, too, is the Bible, when admired only from a distance. We treasure Scripture by taking it down from the shelf and using it! A used Bible increases, rather than decreases, in value.

One way to put the Bible to use is by reading it daily and systematically on an individual basis, and regularly in our worship services. It's ironic that most evangelical churches which profess to treasure the Bible make very little use of it in their services, while churches considered liberal usually make Scripture reading an important part of their services!

We must do more than read the Bible, however. We must interpret it. Some object that interpretation is unnecessary, that by it we replace the work of the Holy Spirit with human effort—as one writer punned, *exegesis* means "exit Jesus." Given how much God involved human beings in the writing of inspired Scripture, though—writing in their own tongues, using metaphors with which they were familiar, copying manuscripts by hand—the truth lies in the other direction. It would, or should, surprise us if we could understand the Bible without the use of human reason, tradition, and experience, if the Holy Spirit just whispered truth in our ears. There can be no right understanding of Scripture without the work of the Holy Spirit in the interpreter; the Spirit uses our efforts to open this treasure to our eyes and hearts. While God's Spirit enables anyone to understand the basic message of sin and salvation, discovering all God has placed in the Scripture requires the skilled work of careful interpretation.

For one thing, the Bible is a collection of many types of ancient literature—law and prophecy, poetry and narrative, and much more. Interpretation reveals what kind of literature we're reading and how the author wanted it to be read. Because the psalmist wrote poems, he used word pictures; he would be offended if we took his metaphors literally, for example, reading about God's wings (Ps. 91:4) and imagining God is a giant bird.

Another reason to interpret the Bible is that it was written in Hebrew, Aramaic, and Greek, rather than English. To translate from one language into another requires interpretation, since most words convey more than one meaning. The translator must decide which words fit best based on the context, a process requiring interpretation.

Not only does the Bible come to us in foreign languages, it comes from foreign lands. The geography of the lands of the Bible is very different from what most of us are familiar with. We consider rain a mixed blessing; we know the farmers need it, but it might mean the cancellation of our ballgame. In a hot, dry climate where infrequent rains meant the difference between life and death, Jesus' promise of rain falling on the just and the unjust is good news indeed.

The culture of ancient Israel is different from ours as well. Our economy depends on manufacturing, service, and information. Ancient Israel depended on subsistence farming. In principle, our society is egalitarian, women and men having equal influence and opportunity. The Bible reflects (but ultimately does not condone) patriarchalism, where men are considered the more important gender. Our society is forward-looking; theirs looked backward, valuing age over youth and placing great stock in one's lineage.

Some differences are more subtle. One of my students, when studying Psalm 46, came to the part that speaks of the sea roaring and foaming. He commented how this verse reminded him of relaxing summers at the beach. Unfortunately, he completely missed what the psalmist was trying to say. People in the ancient world, including Israel, did not have positive feelings about the sea; they feared it as threatening and ominous. So a third reason for interpretation is that it allows us to understand the Bible's geography and culture, making it more likely we'll hear what the biblical author intended to say.

Fourth, we need to interpret because the Bible relies heavily on metaphors, and metaphors are easily misunderstood. If I say, "I'm so hungry I could eat a horse," you know I'm very hungry, but not how much I could eat, and certainly not what I'm hungry for. Metaphors work that way, communicating the general impression with extra force, but lacking precision. Moreover, since God is more different from us than we are from insects, all words about God must be metaphorical: "As a father has compassion on his children, so the LORD has compassion on those who fear him" (Ps. 103:13); "He is the Rock, his works are perfect, and all his ways are just" (Deut. 32:4).

The many passages describing God in physical terms (e.g., hand, eye, back, face) are metaphorical, since God as Spirit has no physical features. We know, too, not to take literally the image of God on a heavenly throne: what would it mean for a Spirit to be seated? Such descriptions are God's way of helping us understand God's sovereignty. Metaphors communicate powerfully, but require interpretation to be understood.

So far, we've argued for interpretation based on the nature of the Bible itself. Let's add one more reason to interpret: us. Interpretation helps ensure we're actually seeing what the Bible says, rather than what we want it to say or what we always thought it said. We cheer Jesus' harsh words to the Pharisees, never asking whether we may be more like Pharisees than we want to admit. We delight in God's promises to the poor and afflicted, without considering whether we may be more like their rich oppressors. Interpretation forces us to listen to Scripture more objectively, and thereby to hear what God is saying to us.

The fact is, in spite of fervent claims to the contrary, no one ever just reads the Bible; everyone reads and interprets. Are we aware of the methods we use and of the assumptions that lie beneath those methods? Are those methods and assumptions appropriate ways to understand the treasure God has given us? Interpretation helps ensure that the answer to these questions is yes.

As important as it is for us to interpret the Bible, we don't really treasure the Bible until we put it to work in our lives. Jesus reserved his harshest words for those who were the Bible scholars of his day, but who failed to put it into action. Interpretation in the Wesleyan tradition insists on taking the truths of God's Word and applying them in practical ways to guide our thoughts and actions as individuals and as a community. We are not content only to know God is sovereign; we must trust this sovereign God in the choices we make. It's not enough to believe humans were created in the image of God. We must treat others with dignity, and insist on this in the church and wider society.

CONCLUSION

A few years ago on the TV program *Antiques Road Show*, a man learned that the tomahawk passed down to him was actually worth more than one hundred thousand dollars. He sheepishly recounted how he had played with it as a child, realizing he could have ruined his treasure. Our treasure is worth much more than one hundred thousand dollars, and ours becomes more valuable with use, not less. By reading, interpreting, and living according to the Bible, we prove its worth, demonstrating our awareness of the treasure we possess, and discovering the riches the Holy Spirit desires to bestow on us.

ACTION/REFLECTION SUGGESTIONS

1. Set aside a time each day when you read a passage of Scripture and listen to the voice of the Holy Spirit as he applies this passage to your specific circumstances. Don't be discouraged if it takes a little while for your hearing to adjust.

2. Research the process by which the Bible came to be translated into English.

3. Read the introductions to several modern translations to discover the translation philosophies employed. Compare and contrast these philosophies.

4. If you are responsible for worship in your church, begin to implement more Scripture reading into your services, perhaps following the lectionary readings located at http://www.lectionary.com.

FOR FURTHER READING

Duvall, J. Scott, and J. Daniel Hays. *Grasping God's Word: A Hands-On Approach to Reading, Interpreting, and Applying the Bible* (2nd ed.). Grand Rapids: Zondervan, 2005.

Scott and Hays explain in elementary fashion how to read the Bible, how to understand its different contexts, and how to arrive at what the Bible means. They also walk the reader through the types of literature found in the Old and New Testaments.

Fee, Gordon D., and Douglas Stuart. *How to Read the Bible for All Its Worth*, (3rd ed). Grand Rapids: Zondervan, 2003.

Fee and Stuart give helpful guidance in why we need to interpret and how to interpret each type of literature found in the Bible. They also provide tips on choosing good translations and commentaries.

Green, Joel. *Seized by Truth: Reading the Bible as Scripture.* Nashville: Abingdon Press, 2007.

Writing as a respected biblical scholar from the greater Wesleyan family, Green offers help in reading the Bible as God's Word. He discusses the roles of the reader's assumptions, resources available, methods employed, and of Scripture as our authority.

Marshall, I. Howard. *Beyond the Bible: Moving from Scripture to Theology.* Grand Rapids: Baker Academic, 2004.

This highly respected Bible scholar candidly and courageously explores how we move from discovering what the Bible says to how we employ it in the formation of theology. It includes responses by two theologians, Kevin Vanhoozer and Stanley E. Porter.

Tate, W. Randolph. *Biblical Interpretation: An Integrated Approach* (rev. ed.). Peabody, Mass.: Hendrickson, 1997.

Tate helps the reader learn to study the world behind the biblical text (bridging the historical, cultural, and linguistic barriers), the world within the text (reading the Bible as literature), and the world in front of the text (what we as readers bring to the text).

NOTES

1. "The Battle of the Books," *The Economist*, http://www.economist.com/world/international/displaystory.cfm?story_id=10311317, accessed February 4, 2009.

2. Woodrow Wilson, "An Address in Denver on the Bible" (address of May 7, 1911, observing the three-hundredth anniversary of the KJV) in *The Papers of Woodrow Wilson*, Vol. 23, 1911–1912, Arthur S. Link, ed. (Princeton, 1977), 15, 11.

3. D. A. Carson, Douglas Moo, and Leon Morris, *An Introduction to the New Testament* (Grand Rapids: Zondervan, 1992), 494.

4. Beverly Carradine, *Better Way* (Cincinnati: God's Revivalist Office, 1896), 244.

5. Neil R. Lightfoot, *How We Got the Bible* (Grand Rapids: Baker, 1988), 92.

6. "A Statistical Summary of Languages with the Scriptures," http://www.biblesociety.org/index.php?id=22, accessed February 4, 2009.

7. Joseph Coleson in an interview with Lawrence Wilson, http://www.lawrencewilson.com/2008/08/do-we-need-more-bibles.html, accessed August 14, 2008.

8. Cited in Richard Lovett, *The Printed English Bible, 1525–1885* (London: The Religious Tract Society, 1909), 169.

JOHN WESLEY'S BIBLE INTERPRETATION PRINCIPLES

Mark L. Weeter

All Scripture is God-breathed and is useful for teaching, rebuking, correcting and training in righteousness, so that the man of God may be thoroughly equipped for every good work.

—2 Timothy 3:16–17

But my own conscience acquits me of having designedly misinterpreted any single passage or having written one line with the purpose of inflaming the hearts of Christians against each other.

—John Wesley

It seems reasonable, in a book discussing a Wesleyan approach to biblical interpretation, to ask, "How did John Wesley interpret Scripture?" This chapter is an introductory answer to that question.

No matter the issue or problem, whether practical or doctrinal, Wesley referred all to the Bible. In a letter to William Dodd in 1756 he stated, "I try every Church and every doctrine by the Bible. This is the word by which we are to be judged in that day."[1] All issues and concerns were to be referred to the Bible, but was Wesley naïve enough to believe all who read the Bible would find the same answers, or find their answers in the same manner? Studying Wesley, one discovers he argued at times with those who rejected Scripture, but at other times with mystics, Calvinists, Roman Catholics, and fellow members of the Church of England—all of whom also referred to the Bible for authority.

Wesley realized if the Bible were to be used, it had to be interpreted. He also realized that obscure and controversial passages are difficult to understand; regardless of purity of motive, error may creep into interpretation. In the sermon "Christian Perfection" (1741), he stated, "Hence even the children of God are not agreed as to the interpretation of many places in Holy Writ; nor is the difference of opinion any proof that they are not the children of God on either side."[2]

WESLEY'S INTERPRETIVE PRINCIPLES

Several principles emerge in Wesley's discussions of his views on biblical interpretation. We may take these as primary rules Wesley followed in his teaching and preaching. The order of these principles, as outlined here, reflects my choice for consistency and order. I do not mean to suggest this order represents Wesley's own prioritizing of them.

INTERPRET SCRIPTURE AIDED BY THE SPIRIT WHO INSPIRED IT

Clearly, Wesley was convinced that God inspired the Scriptures:

"All Scripture is given by the inspiration of God" (2 Tim. 3:16), and herein we are distinguished from Jews, Turks, and Infidels. We believe this written Word of God to be the only and the sufficient rule of Christian faith and practice; and herein we are fundamentally distinguished from those of the Romish Church.[3]

If the Bible was inspired by God, it's consistent to suppose that the Spirit of God would supplement the revelation. Wesley believed that Scripture could be understood only through the same Spirit by whom it was given. In a letter to the bishop of Gloucester in 1762 he wrote, "I do firmly believe (and what serious man does not) we need the same Spirit to understand the Scripture that enabled the holy men of old to write it."[4]

For Wesley, the reading of Scripture was based upon a twofold inspiration. Note his thoughts in his *Explanatory Notes*, commenting on 2 Timothy 3:16: "The Spirit of God not only once inspired those who wrote it, but continually inspires and supernaturally assists those that read it with earnest prayer."[5] A similar statement is found in his book *The Christian's Pattern*, an extracting of *The Imitation of Christ*, where Wesley quoted Thomas à Kempis's guidelines for reading Scripture: "Truth not eloquence is to be sought for in the Holy Scripture. All Scripture is to be read in the same Spirit wherewith it was written."[6] Wesley exhorted his preachers to desire "God's holy inspiration," to "think things that be good," and to "perfectly love Him and worthily magnify His holy name."[7]

To receive such inspiration of the Spirit in biblical interpretation required dedication to meditation and prayer. Wesley also realized dependence on inward revelation could be abused; thus, inspiration did not (and does not) eliminate the need for reason, experience, and tradition in the work of interpretation. Nonetheless, it's safe to say no one prior to Wesley placed such great emphasis on the work of the Holy Spirit in aiding interpretation of Scripture as he did.

What should we conclude from Wesley's emphasis? The interpretation of Scripture is not merely a dry academic exercise of exegesis, and of linguistic, homiletical, and historical studies. It's a living, breathing, event wherein we trust the Holy Spirit of truth to guide us into all truth (John 16:13). Our prayer should be that the same Spirit who inspired the human authors will inspire and guide us in our interpretation. Consider the privilege we have as biblical interpreters. How often have you been studying, or even reading for pleasure, and reached a troubling or difficult section? Wouldn't it be great to be able to phone the author and ask, "What did you mean here? What point were you trying to get across?" We have that opportunity! We can ask the Bible's divine author to "guide us into truth" as we remember that the same "Spirit of God not only once inspired those who wrote it, but continually inspires and supernaturally assists those that read it with earnest prayer."[8]

INTERPRET SCRIPTURE LITERALLY WHEN POSSIBLE

Wesley delineated this principle in a letter to Samuel Furley in 1755. "The general rule of interpreting the Scripture is this: the literal sense of every text is to be taken if it be not contrary to some other texts. But in that case, the obscure text is to be interpreted by those which speak more plainly."[9] Wesley was so convinced of the literalness of Scripture, that he believed that some Scripture has no meaning without this view. In a letter to Mary Bishop in 1776, he stated, "Either the text in Ezekiel 33:8 means literally, or it has no meaning at all . . . But the most decisive of all proofs is Scripture."[10]

Wesley recognized that the literal meaning of Scripture includes figurative language and symbolic passages. (See chapter 7 of this volume.) But like Luther and the Reformers, he was at pains to avoid basing doctrine on allegory and other uncontrolled methods. Along with Wesley's logical bent, this is what led him to emphasize the plain rules of grammar and syntax and to accept the plain, natural meaning of a passage (literal or figurative), unless it led to absurdity, contradicted other Scripture passages, was contrary to reason, or ignored the context. Wesley stated this principle already in 1738, in a letter to Lady Cox. "To anyone who asketh . . . what our principles are, I answer clearly. We have no principles but those revealed in the Word of God. In the interpretation whereof we always judge the most literal sense to be the best, unless the literal sense of one contradicts other Scripture."[11]

INTERPRET SCRIPTURE IN ITS CONTEXT

On a number of occasions Wesley emphasized the importance of examining not only the text, but the context in interpretation. In his long letter to Dr. Warburton, bishop of Gloucester, in 1762, Wesley contended, "My objections to this account are, first it contradicts St. Paul, and secondly it contradicts itself. First, it contradicts Paul. It fixes a meaning upon his words foreign both to text and to context."[12]

Already in his 1727 sermon "On Corrupting the Word of God," Wesley warned against ignoring the narrow context—the immediately preceding and following passages. He contended for explaining Scripture "in the most natural obvious way, by what precedes and what follows the place in question, and commented on by the most sure way, the least liable to mistake or corruption, the producing of parallel places that express the same thing more plainly."[13]

While recognizing Wesley's clear statements concerning the importance of context, it's true, too, that in practice he was predominantly a textual or topical preacher, not an expository preacher. His series of messages "Upon Our Lord's Sermon on the Mount I–XIII" is the closest to an expository series he preached.

Several reasons account for this. First, Wesley viewed the Bible as a whole, both Old and New Testaments, with its various texts as parts of a single theology. Thus, he interpreted according to the "analogy of faith," applied broadly across the whole range of the Scriptures. Second, the primary purpose of Wesley's preaching and teaching was more evangelistic than exegetical. He was concerned with the people he was preaching to—their conversion, then their edification—and at times the tools of the scholar seem subordinated to the note of evangelistic urgency.

Finally, Wesley often used the Scripture for an apologetic purpose. He was very concerned with establishing sound doctrine as he disputed theological positions such as Christian perfection, original sin, and predestination. At times, Wesley approached Scripture more theologically than exegetically and resorted to citing proof texts, a common practice in the eighteenth century. Proof-texting is held in low repute in modern hermeneutical practice, but let's give Wesley the chance to speak for himself: "But my own conscience acquits me of having designedly misinterpreted any single passage or having written one line with the purpose of inflaming the hearts of Christians against each other."[14]

Here, it appears Wesley "preached better than he practiced." Still, we should follow his urging to consider context in interpretation, recognizing the best of intentions will not deliver us from error if we ignore sound hermeneutical principles. Wesley certainly was honest and always strove to use good judgment. But what most helped him avoid interpretive error was his careful consistency in interpreting any particular verse according to the general theme of Scripture.

INTERPRET SCRIPTURE ACCORDING TO SCRIPTURE

In his 1785 sermon "New Creation," Wesley commented:

It must be allowed that after all the researches we can make, still our knowledge of the great truth which is delivered to us in these words is exceedingly short and imperfect. As this is a point of mere revelation, beyond the reach of all our natural faculties, we cannot penetrate far into it, nor form any adequate conception of it. But it may be an encouragement to those who have in any degree tasted of the powers of the world to come, to go as far as we can go, interpreting Scripture by Scripture, according to the analogy of faith.[15]

In the phrasing "interpreting Scripture by Scripture, according to the analogy of faith," we have two closely connected parts of one key interpretive principle. By "the analogy of faith" Wesley meant interpreting Scripture by Scripture's overall doctrinal teaching. Because of his understanding of revelation, Wesley approached the Bible as a whole. The Scripture is not a group of unrelated statements; rather, the wholeness of biblical theology impacts all efforts at biblical interpretation.

Any attempt at biblical interpretation, therefore, must concentrate on the Holy Scriptures as a whole. This idea of the "whole Scriptures" or the "whole analogy of faith" is a favorite metaphor of Wesley, occurring fifteen times in his sermons. A number of "grand truths" run throughout the Bible so that individual passages cannot be interpreted in isolation. We must interpret Scripture by Scripture, by the analogy of faith, if we want to see its interconnectedness. In a 1745 letter to John Smith, Wesley said, "As to the Word of God, you well observe, 'We are not to frame doctrines by the sound of particular texts, but the general tenor of Scripture, soberly studied and consistently interpreted.'"[16]

For Wesley there was no higher authority than Scripture; thus, he clearly agreed with his father's admonition, "You ask me, which is the best commentary on the Bible? I answer, the Bible."[17] In his tract, *Popery Calmly Considered*, Wesley said, "And Scripture is the best expounder of Scripture. The best way therefore to understand it, is carefully to compare Scripture to Scripture, and thereby learn the true meaning of it."[18]

We find in Wesley's 1739 sermon "Free Grace" an extended statement (here abridged) of the reasons why he could not accept a doctrine he judged to contradict the general tenor of Scripture:

And as the doctrine manifestly and directly tends to overthrow the whole Christian revelation, so it does the same thing by plain consequence in making the revelation contradict itself. For it is grounded on such an interpretation of some texts (more or fewer matters not), as flatly contradicts all other texts and indeed the whole scope and tenor of Scripture . . . They contradict the whole oracles of God . . . [This is] an abundant proof that it is not of God.[19]

WESLEY'S LINKAGE OF INTERPRETATION WITH APPLICATION

As mentioned earlier, Wesley's characteristic role was that of a preacher—moreover, not as an exegete, but as an evangelist. While he did not ignore the historical context, he was more concerned with the present application. John Oswalt has referred to Wesley's use of Scripture at times as "illustrative."[20] He used biblical events and statements to illustrate and illuminate the present situation. George Turner observed that Wesley's use of Scripture sometimes resembles Peter's use of the Old Testament at Pentecost, i.e., that the Scripture's illumination of present experience may seem more important than the historical situation it records.[21]

In light of Wesley's emphasis on application in interpretation, we must remind ourselves once again that his purpose was primarily evangelical. The Scripture was his guide; the medium was the sermon. Wesley's main desire was to deliver the truth of the gospel and to see it result in salvation. Thus, he wanted people not only to study the Bible, but also to do something with what they learned. For this, it was necessary that biblical interpretation be made understandable and practicable for the masses of unlearned people. Wesley had little patience with theory for theory's sake:

I design plain truth for plain people. Therefore of set purpose I abstain from all nice and philosophical speculations: from all perplexed and intricate reasonings, and as far as possible from even the show of learning, unless in sometimes citing the original Scriptures. I labour to avoid all words which are not easy to be understood, all which are not used in common life: and in particular those kinds of technical terms that so frequently occur in bodies of divinity, those modes of speaking which men of reading are intimately acquainted with, but which to common people are an unknown tongue.[22]

For Wesley, one read and interpreted the Bible for more than mere enlightenment or understanding; the goal was to understand the application to life. Melvin Dieter has summarized him well: "Wesley would simply say that any pattern of biblical interpretation which does not have the practical result as its immediate goal in life is suspect."[23]

The lessons from Wesley on this point are abundant and clear. Our interpretations, Bible studies, and sermons are not to be opportunities to show how learned we are. Our messages are not to be littered with Greek pronunciations, theological terms, and other examples of our profound vocabulary—until one might wonder if we attempted to cross an unabridged dictionary and fell in! Knowledge for knowledge's sake can be valuable, but in the interpretation of Scripture, our learning is primarily to enable us to declare the message of God simply and clearly. Moreover, the purpose of our proclamation is to encourage and bring about changes in lives—our own and others'.

CONCLUSION

Of course, Wesley was not infallible in his biblical interpretation, any more than in other areas of his life. Still, we can improve our own work of interpretation by consistent practice of Wesley's principles:

1. Pray that God, who inspired the Bible's human writers, will inspire us in interpreting it.

2. Interpret Scripture literally, unless the literal meaning of a text leads to absurdity, is contrary to reason, contradicts its context, or contradicts other Scriptures.

3. Interpret according to context; place no meaning on a text that is contrary either to its historical or immediate (narrow) context.

4. Allow Scripture to interpret Scripture; never interpret a passage in a manner contrary to the teaching of the whole of Scripture.

5. Link interpretation to application; when the truth of Scripture is revealed appropriately and effectively, the result is changed lives.

If we follow these principles Wesley taught us, then perhaps in good conscience we also may describe ourselves as "men and women of one book."

ACTION/REFLECTION SUGGESTIONS

1. Consider how you may begin regularly asking the Holy Spirit to inspire your interpretation each time you approach the Scripture, whether personally or professionally.

2. As you read this book's other chapters, ask yourself how their guidance is grounded in Wesley, and also what we've learned since Wesley's time that improves our interpretational skills and outcomes. How do we continue to make Wesley our partner in interpretation, rather than leave him behind?

3. A little exercise: Wesley said Scripture should be interpreted literally wherever possible. How, then, would you respond to someone who maintains, based on 1 Timothy 3:1–5, first, that clergy should not be paid, and second, that if a clergyperson's child "goes bad," that the clergyperson should leave the ministry?

4. A friend, or someone for whom you have pastoral responsibility, has just read Hebrews 10:26–27 and now comes to you thinking he or she has no possibility of repentance, because he or she willfully sinned after knowing to do better. How would you use the scriptural context (narrow and broad) to help this person understand the true teaching of this passage?

FOR FURTHER READING

Walvoord, John. *Inspiration and Interpretation.* Grand Rapids: Eerdmans, 1957.

This is a classic book on these topics from a more Reformed perspective, but which also deals explicitly with Wesley's views.

Weeter, Mark. *John Wesley's View and Use of Scripture.* Eugene: Wipf and Stock Publishers, 2007.

A similar treatment of the same topics as those addressed in this chapter, but in much more detail.

Wesley, John. *Explanatory Notes upon the New Testament.* London: Epworth Press, 1948; and *A Plain Account of Christian Perfection.* Kansas City: Beacon Hill Press, 1971.

To understand Wesley's views really requires reading his works. These two books will give the reader a good deal of insight into his views on the inspiration and authority of Scripture.

NOTES

1. Nehemiah Curnock, ed., *The Letters of the Reverend John Wesley A.M.*, vol. 3 (London: Charles Kelly, n.d.), 157–58.

2. Albert Outler, ed., *The Works of John Wesley*, vol. 2 (Nashville: Abingdon Press, 1985), 102.

3. Rupert Davies, ed., *The Works of John Wesley*, vol. 9 (Nashville: Abingdon Press, 1989), 33–34.

4. Gerald Cragg, ed., *The Works of John Wesley*, vol. 11 (Nashville: Abingdon Press, 1989), 524.

5. Wesley, *Explanatory Notes upon the New Testament* (London: Epworth Press, 1948), 794.

6. John Wesley, *The Christian's Pattern* (Oxford: Oxford University Press, 1964), 123.

7. Curnock, *Letters*, vol. 4, 44.

8. Wesley, *Explanatory Notes*, 794.

9. Frank Baker, ed., *The Works of John Wesley*, vol. 26 (Oxford: Oxford University Press, 1982), 557.

10. Curnock, *Letters*, vol. 6, 245.

11. Baker, *The Works of John Wesley*, vol. 25 (1980), 533.

12. Curnock, *Letters*, vol. 4, 347.

13. Outler, *The Works of John Wesley*, vol. 4 (1987), 247.

14. Wesley, *Explanatory Notes*, 8.

15. Outler, *The Works of John Wesley*, vol. 2 (1985), 501.

16. Baker, *The Works of John Wesley*, vol. 26 (1982), 158.

17. A. Skevington Wood, *The Burning Heart* (Grand Rapids: Eerdmans, 1967), 136.

18. Thomas Jackson, ed., *The Works of the Rev. John Wesley*, vol. 10 (London: John Mason, 1829), 142.

19. Outler, *The Works of John Wesley*, vol. 3 (1986), 552–54.

20. John Oswalt, "John Wesley's Use of the Old Testament in Doctrinal Teaching," *Wesleyan Theological Journal* 12 (1977), 42.

21. George Allen Turner, *The Vision Which Transforms* (Kansas City: Beacon Hill Press, 1964), 239.

22. Outler, *The Works of John Wesley*, vol. 1 (1984), 104.

23. Melvin Dieter, "Musings," *Wesleyan Theological Journal* 14 (1979), 1.

REASON, TRADITION, AND EXPERIENCE IN BIBLE INTERPRETATION

Mark L. Weeter

Do not conform any longer to the pattern of this world, but be transformed by the renewing of your mind. Then you will be able to test and approve what God's will is—his good, pleasing and perfect will.

—Romans 12:2

It is a fundamental principle with us [the Methodists], that to renounce reason is to renounce religion, that religion and reason go hand in hand, and that all irrational religion is false religion.

—John Wesley

How do you continue a discussion with someone upon discovering you disagree over a theological point or doctrine if you both refer to the Bible as your source of authority? Perhaps John Wesley can help us here. Like many of us, when challenged for authority on a theological question, Wesley appealed first to the Bible. Note his letter to William Dodd: "I therein build on no authority, ancient or modern, but the Scripture. If this supports any doctrine, it will stand; if not, the sooner if falls the better."[1]

But Wesley also knew that quoting Scripture rarely solves any controversial point. Far too often, discussion comes to an impasse of merely citing proof texts, often using the same parts of Scripture! Wesley also recognized that "scarce ever was any heretical opinion either invented or reinvented or revised, but Scripture was quoted to defend it."[2] Therefore, some secondary authority is needed to help in interpreting the Bible.

Wesley's views were greatly influenced by his training in the Anglican tradition. For centuries the Church of England had placed itself under the authority of Scripture as the primary source of discovering God's supreme law. A secondary source was Christian tradition; it never was to be used as a substitute, but neither was the primacy of Scripture meant to preclude appeal to saintly Christians of other ages. Finally, when even Scripture and tradition were not enough, the Church recognized that God has implanted within the human creation the faculty of reason, by which we may make, and recognize as valid, our own interpretations of Scripture. Reason is a gift of God and, though affected by the fall, still operates. Within this Anglican interpretive tradition, Wesley grew up, was educated, and placed himself all his adult life.

But Wesley didn't limit himself to these three. He added another element—Christian experience. Wesley insisted on "heart religion" in the place of normal Christian orthodoxy. This represented something of an innovation on Wesley's part. It's important to understand that Scripture, tradition, reason, and experience combined to help him see experience as a fourth, legitimate element in determining proper interpretation and use of Scripture.

With the addition of this fourth element, we have what has become known as the "Wesleyan Quadrilateral." All four elements have legitimate claims to authority, but it's important to remember they're not equal elements. Used rightly, the Quadrilateral makes reason, tradition, and experience aids in evaluating truth, but never of equal authority with Scripture. Scripture is the primary authority; it's illuminated by the collective light of Christian wisdom through the ages, interpreted best through the discipline of reason, received in the heart, and worked out in life by faith; i.e., Christian experience.

We identify ourselves as Wesleyan. We will benefit from discovering what Wesley taught about reason, tradition, and experience, how we can use them in biblical interpretation, and even about dangers to be avoided.

THE USE OF REASON IN INTERPRETING SCRIPTURE

John Wesley knew it was not sufficient merely to base one's assertions upon the authority of the Bible. Everyone who reads the Bible must interpret it. Correct interpretation requires the use of reason, as Wesley declared in a letter to Dr. Rutherford in 1768. He wrote, "It is a fundamental principle with us (the Methodists), that to renounce reason is to renounce religion, that religion and reason go hand in hand, and that all irrational religion is false religion."[3]

The importance of reason is not that it provides another source of revelation. Ultimately, we can know God only through revelation, which includes: (1) Scripture and, (2) the experience of the inward witness. But reason's role is essential, since only through reason can we make a rational connection between Scripture and experience. Wesley wanted to preclude the manipulation of the principle of "only Scripture" that was exhibited, for example, by the mystics of his day, in ways that open the faith to all manner of unchecked excesses. We see this same problem today with those who say they do not teach or preach "theology or doctrine," but "only the Bible." Clearly, they do not realize theology is merely an understanding of God based on Scripture, and that reason helps us interpret Scripture more, not less, accurately.

The best way to understand Wesley's views on reason is to read his 1781 sermon "The Case for Reason Impartially Considered." In it,

Wesley not only clearly showed that Scripture is foundational, but also that reason is essential for the proper interpretation of Scripture:

> The foundation of true religion stands upon the Oracles of God . . . Now of what excellent use is reason if we would either understand ourselves, or explain to others those living oracles . . . Is it not reason (assisted by the Holy Spirit), which enables us to understand what the Holy Scriptures declare concerning the being and attributes of God? . . . It is by reason that God enables us in some measure to comprehend his method of dealing with the children of men . . . By reason we learn what is that new birth without which we cannot enter into the kingdom of heaven, and what that holiness is, without which no man shall see the Lord. By the due use of reason we come to know what are the tempers implied in inward holiness and what it is to be outwardly holy in all manner of conversation.[4]

Wesley realized the importance of reason in understanding what he called "the Oracles of God." At the same time, he understood that reason is only a "hand-maiden of faith, the servant of revelation."[5] He recognized the danger of the under- or overuse of reason pressed to extremes. Knowing that reason has severe limitations and cannot be trusted alone, Wesley advised, "Let reason do all that reason can: employ it as far as it will go. But at the same time acknowledge it is utterly incapable of giving either faith, or hope or love: and consequently of producing either real virtue or substantial happiness. Expect these from a higher source, even from the Father of the spirits of all flesh."[6]

In an age of tremendous emphasis on preaching to felt needs and looking for the perfect "worship experience," it would be well for us to recognize, as Wesley did, that the use of reason is absolutely essential if doctrine is to avoid being swept away by an overemphasis on enthusiasm and impressions. Note the following warning from Wesley's 1750 sermon "The Nature of Enthusiasm":

> Beware you do not fall into the second sort of enthusiasm fancying you have those gifts of God which you have not. Trust not in visions or dreams, in sudden impressions or strong impulses of any kind. Remember, it is not by these you are to know what is the 'will of God' on any particular occasion, but by applying the plain scriptural rule, with the help of experience and reason, and the ordinary assistance of the Spirit of God.[7]

A former professor of mine shared an incident from his Bible college days. Desiring to be constantly obedient to God, he was running across campus one day in a driving rain storm to reach his next class. In the middle of campus, far from any shelter, he felt "impressed" to stop and pray. He knelt down immediately and started to pray; for several moments he stayed, getting more and more soaked. Then he suddenly realized, "This is stupid. Why would God ask me to do this?" His conclusion: "God the Holy Spirit has common sense, and he expects us to use ours."

John Wesley's conclusion was very similar. God is a rational being; therefore, our interpretation of Scripture should be rational. Reason is not to be driven from the temple of religion as though it had no place in the service of God. Rather, as Wesley stated, "The children of light walk by the joint light of reason, Scripture, and the Holy Ghost."[8]

THE USE OF TRADITION
IN INTERPRETING SCRIPTURE

In "Farther Thoughts on Separation from the Church of England" (1789), Wesley wrote, "From a child I was taught to love and reverence the Scriptures, the oracles of God and next to these to esteem the primitive Fathers, the writers of the first three centuries. Next after the primitive church, I esteemed our own, the Church of England, as the most scriptural national church in the world."[9]

For Wesley, the fundamental authority of Scripture did not necessitate the abandonment of centuries of tradition of the church. Christian tradition was more than a curiosity or a source of illustrative materials; it was a living spring of Christian insight. For some time, he valued the writings of the church fathers, prior to the Council of Nicaea, just below the Scriptures themselves, as "containing pure, uncorrupted doctrine of Christ, and so inspired as to be scarce capable of mistake."[10] Little wonder that during his time at Oxford he earned the nickname, "Mr. Primitive Christianity."[11]

Wesley found the church fathers helpful in interpreting Scripture and was quite unsympathetic to those who did not take them seriously in the history of biblical interpretation. Far from ignoring ancient traditions and authorities, he asserted in the "Preface" to his *Sermons*, "If any doubt still remains, I consult those who are experienced in the things of God, and then the writings whereby, being dead they yet speak. And what I thus learn I teach."[12]

Wesley was willing to check his interpretation of Scripture with the great expositors of the church, but he was not willing to let them be the final authority. On a number of occasions he warned against overemphasizing the teachings of the church against the authority of Scripture. In his essay "Roman Catholicism and Reply" he stated, "As long as we have the Scripture, the Church is to be referred to the Scripture and not the Scripture to the Church; and that, as the Scripture is the best expositor of itself, so the best way to know whether anything be of divine authority, is to apply ourselves to the Scripture."[13]

It is important to recognize the priority of Scripture over church tradition, but at the same time it would be foolish to attempt to do biblical interpretation as though it never had been done before.

Karl Barth made a similar point about theology when he said, "We cannot be the church without taking as much responsibility for the theology of the past as for the theology of the present. Augustine, Thomas Aquinas, Martin Luther, and all the rest are not dead but living. They still speak and demand a hearing."[14] By the same token, how arrogant of us, if we were to assume we alone know the answers and could refuse to listen to those who "being dead . . . yet speak."

I once read that we should approach our studies as though we were in a great seminar surrounded by friends in various corners of the room, also laboring to understand the Scriptures. In one corner we find Augustine and Athanasius discussing the Trinity; in another, St. Patrick and Zinzendorf noting the power of light over darkness. Here we find Phoebe Palmer and John Wesley speaking of the power of holiness, while there we see Karl Barth and Charles Wesley discoursing on how to sing praises to God. Pope Gregory the Great speaks on the duties of the pastor, while Martin Luther expounds on justification by faith. If we wish to know the will of God revealed in Scripture, we should study for ourselves, but remember also that the questions we ask have been asked before by more saintly ones than we! As Wesley advised, "The esteeming of the writings of the first three centuries not equally, but next to the Scriptures, never carried any man yet into dangerous errors, nor probably ever will. But it has brought many out of dangerous errors."[15]

THE USE OF EXPERIENCE IN INTERPRETING SCRIPTURE

As noted in the chapter introduction, Wesley added "Christian experience" to the Anglican triad of Scripture, reason, and tradition, as aids to biblical interpretation. George Cell, in his book *The Rediscovery of John Wesley*, states, "It is safe to say that no other teacher of the Christian church and preacher of the gospel ever laid upon experience so heavy a burden of responsibility for discerning and confirming the truth-values of the Christian faith."[16]

This emphasis on Christian experience centered in Wesley's own spiritual struggles. Confronted with interpretations of certain portions of Scripture, Wesley wished to examine conduct as well as verbal profession/witness, i.e., the possibilities seen, as well as claimed, in his contemporaries to verify whether a given interpretation were true to life. A stellar example is Peter Bohler's instruction concerning justification by faith and the assurance of forgiveness of sin. After being shown the Scripture would bear such an interpretation, Wesley still asked, "Are there any whose Christian experience can support such an interpretation?"[17]

For Wesley, the mere assertion of the authority of Scripture and tradition was never adequate. He needed to see their authority conferred upon them by the Holy Spirit. He wished for experience to drive the interpreter back to the Scripture, to see if he or she understood it aright. Wesley was convinced that experience, whether contemporary or ancient, clarifies and confirms Scripture, but does not supersede it.

In considering the relationship between Scripture, reason, and experience, the best term for experience may be *confirmatory*. For Wesley, if a particular interpretation is not born out by the evidence of experience, the interpretation must be wrong. This was an important argument in, for example, his doctrine of perfection. Conversely, if a particular experience does not follow a scriptural pattern—e.g., if an individual's claim to be justified does not issue in the fruits of a holy life—then the experience is invalid.

We should note, also, that for Wesley no single, individual experience could stand alone. Harold Lindstrom, in his book *Wesley and Sanctification*, stated that for Wesley, Christian experience is not simply the experience of the individual, but also the experience of the fellowship.[18] People who were individualists in their thinking were to go beyond their own faith and fears to the one great witness of the universal church in all ages.

Isabel Rivers summarized Wesley's view: "The individual knows God through Scripture and experience. He can readily compare the two; but he also needs the testimony of others, partly in order to test whether his own experience coheres with common experience, and is not particular to himself, and is hence valid, and partly to encourage him to perseverance."[19] Seeing the close connection between experience and Scripture, it's not surprising to find in Wesley's works this typical phrase: "All experience as well as Scripture shows."[20]

Consider how Wesley used experience to confirm Scripture, regarding the doctrine of Christian perfection. He was convinced of the attainability of perfection, but needed to see it as consistent with experience, as well as with Scripture. Wesley therefore tested the experiences of his converts who professed the experience of perfect love, to test the exegesis of the passages he believed support the doctrine. The reason was simple, as he stated in his *Plain Account of Christian Perfection*, "If I were convinced that none in England had attained what has been so clearly and strongly preached by such a number of preachers, in so many places for so long a time, I should be clearly convinced that we had all mistaken the meaning of those Scriptures."[21] For Wesley, experience was not an independent source of doctrine, but could confirm a biblical doctrine, or correct a doctrine thought to be biblical.

Wesley also realized how easily personal experience as a standard of doctrinal truthfulness can be abused. He recognized the tremendous variety in religious experience and knew that no one experience can be considered normative. Therefore, all experience must be submitted to the final authority of Scripture. His fundamental precept on this is defined in a 1748 letter to Thomas Whitehead: "The Scriptures are the touchstone whereby Christians examine all real or supposed revelations. For though the Spirit is our principle leader, yet He is not our rule at all; the Scriptures are the rule whereby He leads us into all truth."[22]

Here, Wesley was responding to his concern about the Quakers making Scripture a "secondary rule subordinate to the Spirit." He also warned against the mystics, who had made a great impression on his early life, for their emphasis on experience and impressions above the Scriptures. Wesley warned against enthusiasm, which may be defined (for his time) as allowing one's religious experience to run contrary to the Word of God. For Wesley, to depart from the Word of God, even based on experience, was to depart from God.

Even with these cautions, Wesley did more to include and legitimize experience as a confirming factor in biblical interpretation than any other biblical scholar, and it is well he did. Ultimately, personal experience with God makes the Scriptures real to us, and keeps our Bible study from being merely an academic exercise.

A young lady bought a book at a local bookstore. She tried several times to read it, but couldn't get past the halfway point; finally, she put it aside and forgot it. Several years later, she began dating a reporter for a local magazine. One evening, she became aware he had authored a book, and it dawned on her which book it was. She rushed home, pulled her dusty volume off the shelf, and read through the night. In the morning, when she finished, she was convinced it was the greatest novel ever written. What made the difference? Was the book any better than when she had started it before? Of course not; there was only one difference. This time she was in love with the author.

Our personal experience with God and with God's people makes the Scriptures come alive to us, and can confirm (or correct) our interpretations. This is a tremendous value, as long as we remember our experiences should never contradict Scripture. As Wesley said, "But will any lover of the Scriptures allow the possibility of this, that the Spirit should ever speak a syllable to any man beside what He publically speaks there [in the Bible]?"[23]

CONCLUSION

In the Wesleyan Quadrilateral—Scripture, reason, experience, and tradition—Wesley sought a balance, with Scripture as the supreme foundational authority, but with no other source of authority neglected. To employ another metaphor, Scripture is the central focus; reason, tradition, and experience are interpretive lenses through which we understand it better. In our efforts, which of us would not benefit from acquaintance with the wisdom of the early church, from education and experience in reason and logical analysis, and from a vital inward faith that transforms the interpretation of Scripture from merely an academic exercise into real personal study? For accurate biblical interpretation, we dare not choose the Bible *or* tradition, reason, and experience. Wesleyans interpret the Bible by the proper use of reason, tradition, and experience.

ACTION/REFLECTION SUGGESTIONS

1. As you read the other chapters of this book, consider how they promote the use of tradition, reason, and experience in biblical interpretation. What specific steps can you take to improve your interpretive practice and skills? How will you build in accountability?

2. Wesley believed in tradition as a valid guide in interpretation of Scripture. For much of the church's history, allegory was a common interpretive method. Even Paul interpreted Old Testament passages allegorically a few times in his epistles. Does this mean Scripture and tradition encourage us to interpret Scripture allegorically today? Why or why not? How do reason and experience, along with Scripture and tradition, inform your answer?

3. A little exercise: You explain to your Sunday school class that bibliomancy, the practice of opening the Bible and haphazardly putting down a finger for divine guidance, isn't a good way to use the Scripture. One of your key members replies that in his experience this method has always been very helpful. How would you respond?

FOR FURTHER READING

Hall, Christopher. *Reading Scripture with the Church Fathers.* Downers Grove, Ill.: InterVarsity, 1998.

Oden, Thomas, ed. *Ancient Christian Commentary on the Scripture.* Downers Grove, Ill.: InterVarsity, 1998–2009.

These are two good collections of ancient Christian primary (original) sources, immensely valuable to the interpreter wanting to know what ancient church tradition actually is and says.

McCown, Wayne, and James Massey, eds. *Interpreting God's Word for Today: An Inquiry into Hermeneutics from a Biblical, Theological Perspective.* Anderson, Ind.: Warner Press, 1982.

As the name implies, this book is a good study of hermeneutical principles with a look at Wesley as well. It was written by scholars in the Wesleyan theological tradition, for Wesleyans.

Weeter, Mark. *John Wesley's View and Use of Scripture.* Eugene, Ore.: Wipf and Stock, 2007.

Wesley's regard for and ways of interpreting Scripture, together with the development of his thinking and practices in the use of tradition, reason, and experience—in short, the topics of this and the previous chapter—I deal with in much more detail in this book.

Wesley, John. A study of his works and journals on these topics is well worth any interpreter's time. You could begin with the sermons, tracts, and books quoted or referred to in these two chapters, and the rest of this book.

Wood, A. Skevington. *The Burning Heart.* Grand Rapids: Eerdmans, 1967.

One of the best theological biographies of Wesley I have read.

NOTES

1. John Telford, ed., *The Letters of the Reverend John Wesley, A.M.*, vol. 3 (London: Epworth Press, 1931), 157–58.

2. Albert Outler, ed., *The Works of John Wesley*, vol. 4 (Nashville: Abingdon Press, 1987), 247.

3. Rupert Davies, ed., *The Works of John Wesley*, vol. 9 (Nashville: Abingdon Press, 1989), 282.

4. Outler, *Works*, vol. 2 (1985), 592–93.

5. Nehemiah Curnock, ed., *The Journals of the Reverend John Wesley, A.M.*, vol. 5 (London: Charles Kelly, n.d.), 492.

6. Outler, *Works*, vol. 2 (1985), 588.

7. Ibid., 59.

8. Telford, *Letters*, vol. 3 (1931), 158.

9. Davies, *Works*, vol. 9 (1989), 538.

10. Thomas Jackson, ed., *The Works of the Reverend John Wesley, A.M.*, vol. 14 (London: John Mason, 1829), 223.

11. Frank Baker, *John Wesley and the Church of England* (London: Epworth Press, 1970), 34.

12. Outler, *Works*, vol. 1 (1984), 106.

13. Jackson, *Works*, vol. 10 (1829), 94.

14. Karl Barth, *Die protestantische Theologie im 19. Jahrhundert* (Zurich: Evangelischer Verlag, 1952), 3.

15. Telford, *Letters*, vol. 2 (1931), 325.

16. George Croft Cell, *The Rediscovery of John Wesley* (New York: Henry Holt and Company, 1935), 71–72.

17. Reginald Ward and Richard Heitzenrater, eds., *The Works of John Wesley*, vol. 18 (Nashville: Abingdon Press, 1988), 248.

18. As quoted in Benjamin Garrison, "Vital Interaction: Scripture and Experience, John Wesley's Doctrine of Authority," *Religion in Life*, 25 (1956), 569.

19. Isabel Rivers, "John Wesley and the Language of Scripture, Reason and Experience," *Prose Studies* 4 (Dec., 1981), 261.

20. Outler, *Works*, vol. 3 (1986), 204.

21. John Wesley, *A Plain Account of Christian Perfection* (Kansas City: Beacon Hill Press, 1971), 67.

22. Telford, *Letters*, vol. 2 (1931), 117.

23. Telford, *Letters*, vol. 3 (1931), 234.

THE UNITY AND COHERENCE OF SCRIPTURE

Kenneth Schenck

The one who loves has fulfilled all other Law . . . If any other
commandment exists, it is summed up in this statement:
"You will love your neighbor as yourself."

—Romans 13:8–9 (author's translation)

[E]very doubtful scripture interpreted according to the grand
truths which run through the whole.

—John Wesley

Wesleyans believe the Bible has a coherent message. Behind this deceptively simple affirmation lies a host of complex issues and perspectives of which, ironically, those who affirm the coherence of Scripture may not even be aware. In what way do the various books of the Bible cohere with each other? We find more than one perspective on this question, not only within the history of Christianity, but even within the history of the Wesleyan movement itself, from Wesley to the present.

Wesley himself principally found the coherence of Scripture by way of what he called the "analogy of faith," in which the several parts of Scripture are aligned with an overarching sense of Christian doctrine. But since Wesley's day, we have had Wesleyan revivalists, Wesleyan dispensationalists, Wesleyan fundamentalists, and Wesleyan evangelicals. Needless to say, these variations make it difficult to pinpoint exactly what a Wesleyan understanding of Scripture's coherence may be.

In the end, it remains for us in the Wesleyan tradition to define scriptural coherence for our generation, in dialogue with our past. This is a good moment to look back at our history and see dynamics to our thought that we may not have been able to see previously. In this chapter, we will show some of the paradigms of coherence our tradition has used, whether knowingly or not. We will conclude with a suggestion for what a Wesleyan sense of Scripture's coherence may be in the days to come.

JOHN WESLEY AND SCRIPTURAL COHERENCE

Wesley's mechanism for organizing diverse biblical material was the "analogy of faith." His *Notes* on Romans 12:6 give a good sense of how it worked for him:

> "Let us prophesy according to the analogy of faith"—St. Peter expresses it, "as the oracles of God"; according to the general tenor of them; according to that grand scheme of doctrine which is delivered therein, touching original sin, justification by faith, and present, inward salvation. There is a wonderful analogy between all these; and a close and intimate connexion between the chief heads of that faith "which was once delivered to the saints." Every article therefore concerning which there is any question should be determined by this rule; every doubtful scripture interpreted according to the grand truths which run through the whole.[1]

The analogy of faith is the coherence of the several parts of Scripture with the "grand scheme of doctrine," the "grand truths which run through the whole." It's a reflection of "a close and intimate connexion between the chief heads of that faith 'which was once delivered to the saints.'"

What Wesley is talking about here is an overarching biblical theology. The "grand scheme of doctrine," for him, was his signature *ordo salutis*, the path to salvation. It included such teachings as those "on original sin, justification by faith, and present, inward salvation." Wesley was by no means the first to speak of a "rule of faith" as an organizing principle for the various materials of the Bible. We find this idea as early as Irenaeus in the late second century. From one perspective, it's the idea that certain core Christian beliefs provide a general rule that governs how the meaning of Scripture is understood and applied. The coherent message of the Bible for Wesley was "the way to heaven." "In His presence I open, I read His book; for this end, to find the way to heaven."[2]

The centuries since Wesley have seen incredible advancement in our understanding of how context determines meaning. Nowhere has the result been more striking than in recent studies in the cultural anthropology of the biblical worlds. Such studies illustrate powerfully that the words of the Bible took on their meanings within the symbolic universes of their ancient cultures. These were cultural networks of meaning based on interrelated customs, paradigms, religious expressions and practices, and societal relationships. We can translate a Hebrew word as "clean" or "unclean" in English. What is nearly impossible to translate is the meaning of these terms within the sociocultural matrix of ancient Israel, the deep significance of such words in their original context.

Wesley, of course, did not have the benefit of such studies. His primary goal was not to determine what the biblical texts meant in their original contexts. Instead, he brought a faith structure to these texts, and this faith structure served as a mechanism for assigning significance to them. That is not to say that the "surface structure" of the text, the way the words themselves seem to interrelate as words, could not impact Wesley's faith structure. But the primary context of biblical words for Wesley was his theological system, not the ancient Near East or the ancient Mediterranean.

Thus, we may say the coherence of Scripture for Wesley came primarily from the theological standpoint he took toward the text, as much as from the text itself. To be sure, the primary content of Wesley's faith structure drew more from the words of Scripture than from any other source. But the organizing principle of those Scriptures came from Wesley's faith, and the content of Scripture was interpreted with reference to that faith structure.

WESLEYAN REVIVALISTS AND DISPENSATIONALISTS

After we have looked at Wesley's hermeneutic, we must pause to remember that the Wesleyan tradition for which this book is written relates to John Wesley more as a grandparent than as a parent. We refer here to the Wesleyan traditions which largely formed their identities in the Holiness revivals of the late 1800s: Wesleyans, Nazarenes, Free Methodists, and others. For us in these traditions, a "Wesleyan" hermeneutic can't simply turn to John Wesley for precedent; we at least must consider also the hermeneutic of our revivalist parents—even if only to dismiss it.

These groups were, by and large, far less overtly theological and intellectual in their focus than was Wesley himself. Their focus was much more practical and experiential, taking the form of their American frontier context. What literature these movements produced in the late 1800s and early 1900s was largely of a popular nature. To be sure, they founded many colleges around the turn of the century. But they founded them primarily to shield their children from broader currents in American culture. They established them to teach the right interpretations of Scripture; i.e., the ways the various groups interpreted it, which were largely of a piece within the revivalist movement.

Thus, the organizing principle the revivalists brought to Scripture was the cluster of distinct ideological perspectives that accompanied their rise as social groups. This perspective included, to be sure, a version of Wesley's theology as nineteenth century America had transformed it, not least through Phoebe Palmer's proclamation of a "shorter way" to the experience of entire sanctification. But it also included elements of the broader Christian culture of their times. They aligned themselves with Prohibition, along with others who were reacting in part, perhaps, to the influx of Irish Catholics into America. They developed traditions around what it meant to keep the Sabbath, how to dress, and what sorts of social activities a Christian could engage in. These traditions had much more to do with the dynamics of their social situations than they did with Wesley.

If the changes Holiness denominations have made to their polities are an indication, the Wesleyan tradition has more and more acknowledged the cultural nature of many of these understandings. This is not necessarily to say our forebears did not accurately hear the Holy Spirit speaking to them in the late 1800s and early 1900s. It is to say they did not so much draw these traditions out of Scripture, as they brought their sense of the Holy Spirit's leading to the Scriptures. For example, few Wesleyan scholars today would suggest the wine Jesus drank was somehow unfermented, though such a view was the emphatic interpretation of our common past. Those in the Wesleyan tradition who continue to favor complete abstinence do so, not because they believe the Bible demands it, but because they believe it coheres better with a holy life in our world today.

It has been easy for some to dismiss this phase of our existence, including these then-common hermeneutical (mis)understandings. However, we should recognize this hermeneutical model is not completely unlike the way some New Testament authors interpreted the Old Testament. For example, in Galatians Paul apparently was in dialogue with individuals who were teaching the Galatians that the promised blessing to Abraham was only "to his seed." We may assume they were teaching that, to be right with God, male Galatian believers would need to join Abraham's seed by being circumcised. In a fantastic exegetical move, Paul pointed out that the word *seed* in Genesis 12:7 is singular, not plural (Gal. 3:16). This seed, Paul boldly proclaimed, does not refer to the many genealogical descendents of Abraham, but to the singular Christ. Those who are in Christ are the true seed of Abraham!

Paul did not draw this interpretation of Genesis out of the biblical text. He came to the text with a truth revealed to him by the Spirit, and found it there. Accordingly, this sort of interpretive method would not receive high marks in a typical inductive Bible study class at an evangelical Christian college or seminary today. Those who dismiss and denigrate the interpretive methods of the nineteenth- and twentieth-century revivalist tradition should recognize they are, at least implicitly, rejecting some of the interpretive patterns found in the New Testament itself.

The twentieth century also saw the impact of dispensationalist thinking on various parts of the Holiness Movement. The organizing principle here was a distinct perspective on history, with our current age as the "end times" of the biblical story. Once again, this organizing principle was as much (or more) brought to the text as induced from the biblical text. For Wesley, the organizing principle was the common faith of Christian history, supplemented by his particular Protestant understanding. For dispensationalists, the coherency was a theological tapestry they wove together from quite diverse contexts into an ingenious synthesis revealing what soon must take place.

Again, we should not be too critical of this stream of Wesleyan thought. We will not convince any Jewish scholars today that Jesus is the Messiah by weaving together Old Testament Scriptures in the way the New Testament authors did. At point after point, we find the New Testament authors read the Old Testament far more "spiritually" than contextually. In a good many passages, the Old Testament proclaims a descendent of David will reign forever, but it did not literally anticipate the significant "messianic upgrade" found in Jesus Christ. With the eyes of the Holy Spirit, the New Testament authors saw much more in the texts of the Old Testament than the original audiences of those texts would have, or could have.

WESLEYAN FUNDAMENTALISTS AND EVANGELICALS

By far the dominant hermeneutical paradigm among Wesleyan Bible scholars today is the evangelical, contextual one. It is based on "inductive Bible study," whose aim is to let the biblical texts mean what they originally meant when they were first written. This evangelical paradigm itself was not birthed without pain. It represents a sort of equilibrium reached by those who continued to affirm the authority and inspiration of Scripture, after they were confronted by the rise of those who read the Bible as a piece of literature (albeit, a great one) like any other book.

Prior to the modern age, Christians certainly presumed the stories in the Bible happened more or less exactly as they are presented. But they rarely were forced to defend—or even to examine—this assumption. Then the rise of historical-critical interpretation not only forced the issue, it often forced it in a hostile way. In America, this was because the historical-critical methodology accompanied the rapid secularization of the nation in the post-Civil War period. The roots of American fundamentalism lie in the vigorous first responses to these challenges. New words were introduced into the hermeneutical conversation, words like "infallible" and "inerrant." These words were formed with a view to defending the truthfulness and the historicity of the biblical stories, as well as to meeting new challenges arising from science.

Some Wesleyans rode this tide of culture, as well, and adopted a fundamentalist approach to biblical coherency. However, this approach also is not without problems, not least because it makes historicity the "be all and end all" of Scriptural coherency. For example, aiming to show the coherency of the Bible in his book *The Battle for the Bible*, Harold Lindsell suggested Peter may have denied Jesus six times—three times before the cock crowed once, and three times before it crowed a second time.[3] The unintended consequence is that the resulting "coherent history" stands far more in tension with the biblical texts, than the various biblical texts themselves stood in tension with each other in the first place!

The evangelicalism of the late twentieth century generally had a more sophisticated understanding of context than did its fundamentalist cousin, not least in relation to ancient genres. It recognized that the books of the Bible were inspired largely within the cultural categories of their original authors and audiences. Accordingly, it's at least potentially inappropriate to apply modern standards of historical precision to the biblical narratives, or to read various texts as though they were speaking directly to contemporary scientific issues. The result has been a complex hermeneutic for appropriating the biblical text today.

First, one must determine the specific meaning a text had originally. The Bible consists of sixty-six books written over a period of about a thousand years in three different languages. The meaning of the words of each individual book is a function of the way words were being used in the specific time and place when it was authored, within the specific symbolic universes of each context. Furthermore, those words took on the specific connotations of the often unique situations they addressed. Read in the light of their original meanings, the Bible is not one book, but a library of very diverse books written in several distinct genres to audiences that died a long time ago.

As the biblical theology debate has shown, inducing a common theological perspective from these diverse texts has been anything but easy when each is read in its full uniqueness. Reading these books in context leads us toward a progressive understanding of revelation in which the New Testament authors understood more than the Old Testament authors. Perhaps we're on the verge of admitting we still may have fallen short of a fully Christian understanding of the New Testament if we had not had the benefit of the Trinitarian and Christological debates of the early Christian centuries.

In the end, inductive Bible study alone cannot give us the coherent Christian perspective on Scripture that we affirm. After all, James did not include a footnote at James 2:24, "a person is justified by works and not by faith alone," explaining how this statement coheres with Romans 3:28, "a person is justified by faith and not by works of law" (author's translations). Whether we like it or not, we are forced to take these two diverse biblical comments and work out a unified perspective that can accommodate both of them. We do this work of integration by assuming a unified stance in relation to the biblical text as a whole. We draw the principal elements of this unified stance from the materials of the Bible itself, but the stance must be, *de facto*, one assumed from outside the Bible looking in. We have no other choice; we can do no other.

WESLEY FOR THE TWENTY-FIRST CENTURY?

What, therefore, might a Wesleyan hermeneutic of scriptural coherence be for the twenty-first century? We're actually in a great position to suggest a way forward that acknowledges the strengths of each of these moments in our history, while appropriating them more reflectively. We might begin by acknowledging the evangelical perspective as far as it goes. We can affirm that all the biblical writings were inspired by God to their original contexts, within the limits of their particular situations and symbolic universes. From this perspective, we see the story of God's revelation of the books of the Bible within history, rather than reverting to the premodern perspective that sees the history of God's revelation within the stories of the Bible.

But we also recognize, with eyes wide open, that we bring to the contents of the biblical texts themselves a rule of faith that God has worked out in the church, as well as a sense of an overall story of the relationship between God and his people throughout the ages. The rule of faith is the common faith of Christendom, formulated as the Holy Spirit has helped the church reflect on the contents of Scripture. Our sense of the story leads us to see the books of the "Jewish Bible" as the Old Testament, rather than as the final statement of God's relationship with his people. Our common faith leads us to give priority to readings of the New Testament text that see Jesus as fully God and fully human, of one substance with the Father. We read the contents of the Bible as an analogy to this rule of faith, as Wesley did, and we unify the diverse texts of the Bible within the Christian story of salvation's history.

Finally, we assert that the Holy Spirit has raised up the people called "Wesleyan" to play an appointed role within the larger body of Christ. We believe he has graced us with important pieces of the puzzle of Christian truth and practice for our world today. We, more than most other Christian groups, take seriously the New Testament's teaching on victory over the power of sin. We are champions of an optimistic understanding of grace, in a Christian culture more focused on a pessimistic understanding of humanity. Indeed, our tradition may have more potential to reconcile the best elements of the Catholic and Protestant traditions than almost any other group. We share much of our hermeneutic in common with the rest of Christendom. The uniqueness of the coherence we find in Scripture comes from the unique aspects of our faith that we bring as a tradition to the biblical texts.

ACTION/REFLECTION SUGGESTIONS

1. What paradigm best summarizes your own approach to integrating Scripture: the revivalist, the fundamentalist, the evangelical, the ancient-future one now developing, or some other? When you've finished reading this volume, reconsider the question. Has your answer changed in any way? Should anything in your answer change?

2. Set aside time over the next few weeks to consider and identify the interpretive paradigm of your local church, including its leadership. Has your church consciously adopted this approach to integrating Scripture, or has it inherited it—"caught it" from its particular tradition or Christian environment?

3. Can you identify a rule of faith you use when you read Scripture, a set of guidelines for how you fit the various parts of the Bible together? What clear verses do you use to help you process unclear ones that seem to conflict with them? Do some soul-searching to identify what drives your choices of which verses you consider clear. Is it your Christian tradition? The common faith of Christianity? Cultural common sense? Something else?

4. Take a moment to reflect on your attitudes toward others. Do you hide behind any specific passage(s) of Scripture to justify less than loving attitudes or actions toward your neighbors and enemies in the world? If so, what do you intend to do about it?

FOR FURTHER READING

Augustine. *On Christian Doctrine.* Widely available.

In this famous treatise, Augustine discussed how to read Scripture through the eyes of the rule of faith and the law of love. Christian interpreters of the Bible should be familiar with it.

Davis, Ellen, and Richard Hays. *The Art of Reading Scripture.* Grand Rapids: Eerdmans, 2003.

This collection of essays presents some of the best current thinking on how Christians read Scripture as a complete, whole, and coherent story.

Green, Joel. *Seized by Truth: Reading the Bible as Scripture.* Nashville: Abingdon Press, 2007.

Green emphasizes reading the Bible, not as a frog to dissect, but as God's living Word to believers of all generations. Rather than fragmenting it, our interpretive work ultimately should reveal the Bible holistically, in its own integrity.

Schenck, Kenneth. *A Brief Guide to Biblical Interpretation.* Marion, Ind.: Triangle Publishing, 2008.

This short guide focuses on two major aspects of serious biblical study: (1) the traditional "original meaning" interpretation; and (2) reading the Bible as one book, i.e., how to integrate into a coherent whole our understanding of the multiple, diverse parts that make up the Christian Scriptures.

Wolterstorff, Nicholas. *Divine Discourse: Philosophical Reflections on the Claim That God Speaks.* Cambridge: Cambridge University Press, 1995.

Woltersdorff argues that Scripture as a whole is divine speech in which God not only says things but does things. It will repay handsomely your effort in reading it.

NOTES

1. John Wesley, *Explanatory Notes upon the New Testament*, "Romans 12:6," available in many editions.

2. John Wesley, *Sermons on Several Occasions*, "Preface, Paragraph 5," 1746.

3. Harold Lindsell, *The Battle for the Bible* (Grand Rapids: Zondervan, 1976), 174–76.

PART 2

A TOOLKIT FOR INTERPRETING SCRIPTURE

GENRE

Kelvin Friebel

Like a lame man's legs that hang limp
is a proverb in the mouth of a fool.
—Proverbs 26:7

Our awareness of genre programs our encounter with a biblical text,
telling us what to look for and how to interpret what we see.
—Leland Ryken

The cartoon strip *Get Fuzzy* is about a young fellow (Rob Wilco),
his dog (Satchel Pooch), and cat (Bucky Katt). In one sequence,
Bucky Katt is standing in front of the television, saying, "This is such a
stupid show . . ." In the next frame he says, "The plot is the same every
single time!" In the last frame, as he is still watching, he comments,
"Oh! Now here she goes floppin' around on the floor again! *Get a writer,
you hack!*" Rob, peering through the door at Bucky Katt, declares,
"Dude, that's an exercise program."[1]

This cartoon illustrates that recognizing and understanding genre and
genres is one of the essential building blocks for proper communication

to take place. We laugh at Bucky Katt because he misunderstood the genre of the television program he was watching, so he expected something quite different from what that program type is designed to offer. Similarly, the danger exists when we interpret a biblical text whose literary type (genre) we may not recognize. We may end up misconstruing the content because we're not reading it based on the rules of that particular genre.

ALL COMMUNICATION INVOLVES GENRE

Genre is foundational to all communication events, regardless of the medium through which the message is transmitted. This is true whether the message is written (a story in a book, a text message on a cell phone, an e-mail on a computer), spoken (a radio program, an academic lecture, a sermon), or audiovisual (a television show, a movie, a stage play). When watching television we recognize the differences between the genres of sit-com, newscast, documentary, game show, sports broadcast, exercise program, late-night talk show, reality show, or criminal investigation show. Being aware of the multiplicity of genres we encounter highlights the fact that communication cannot occur without the use of genres. Since the Bible records God's communication with us, when reading it, we need to take into account that it was written employing genres that were familiar to the people during the times when its various parts were composed. It's impossible to overemphasize the importance of this reality and interpretive principle.

The description of any genre comes from identifying the shared, distinctive characteristics within similar texts that result in their being grouped together. If I gave you a large number of prose texts and asked you to sort them, it wouldn't take long for you to recognize that a number of them have similar, recurring features.

One group of stories you would separate from the others because they all begin with the line, "Once upon a time, in a land, far, far away . . . ," and end with a line such as, ". . . and they lived happily ever after." The content of these stories is fanciful, often involving princes and princesses, and usually draws some type of moral lesson at the end. You would realize that the details of these stories are very different, yet on an abstracted level, they share general characteristics or components. Thus we group them together as being the same genre, which we have labeled "fairy tale."

By the same token, you would recognize some short, pithy sayings as "proverbs," and others as "knock-knock jokes." You would identify one table of figures in the newspaper as baseball scores, and another as daily closing stock prices on Wall Street.

GENRE INVOLVES FORM, CONTENT, FUNCTION, AND SETTING

When we compare various genres, we recognize that their differences are evident both in the elements of the content included, and in the sequences in which those components are arranged. Moreover, different genres have quite different purposes with respect to the results they are attempting to achieve. So any particular genre is identified and described based on three aspects: (1) the form, the external formatting, of how it is said; (2) the content, the constituting components, of what is said; and (3) the function, the persuasive purpose, of why it is said.

Let's take, for example, a classified ad for a used car. The external format of the ad is that it's written in phrases, rather than complete sentences, and overall, it's very brief. It usually only has a couple of lines. With respect to content, although the details given for each specific car are radically different, the thousands of classified ads are virtually identical with respect to the basic constituting elements: the year and make of the car, technical details such as the mileage or condition, asking price, and a phone number of the seller. The persuasive purpose of the genre is to sell the car.

Similarly, the uniqueness of each genre used in the Bible is identified by those three aspects of form, content, and purpose. For example, lament psalms, such as Psalms 13, 22, 42, and 43, are written in the form of poetry, and they usually contain three elements: (1) lament, including very emotional descriptions of the psalmists' distressing situations; (2) petition, voicing the psalmists' requests for God's help in the particular situations; and (3) statement of confidence and trust, affirming the psalmists' assurance that God will help. The life settings out of which lament psalms arise are times of distress and trouble. Their purpose is to voice the psalmists' feelings of anxiety, discouragement, abandonment, and fear, as well as their requests for God to intervene—all from a stance of faith in God.

As noted with lament psalms, genres are frequently linked with particular life settings which give rise to their creation and use; moreover, they're frequently tied to channels of communication common or specific to where they occur. For example, a classified ad is written when one wants to sell something and is found in a printed or on-line newspaper. You would not expect to find a classified ad in the white pages of a telephone book. Similarly, an obituary occurs when someone has died, and also occurs in a printed or on-line newspaper. Although it's more difficult to ascertain specific life-settings for some biblical genres, the life context can be spoken of in general terms. For example, proverbs are tied both to the family life setting of parent-child instruction, and to royal court contexts of training scribes and other administrative functionaries. The psalms functioned within several worship contexts, being used both in private worship and in the more ritualized corporate worship of the temple.

HOW GENRES WORK

GENRES PROVIDE THE FRAMEWORK FOR INTERPRETING COMMUNICATION

Since genre determines the framework for understanding meaning, the first task in interpreting any message is to recognize its genre. For example, you come home and find a piece of paper on the kitchen table. There are five words written on it in a descending column: *butter, milk, peanuts, flour, chocolate.* It obviously falls into the broad genre category of "list." Yet a further genre breakdown—what kind of list is it?—also is necessary for you to understand it. Is this a "shopping list," left for you to go to the store to get these items? Is it part of a "recipe list" of ingredients for the chocolate chip cookies you want to bake? Is it a "spelling list" for your elementary school child to review for her spelling test tomorrow? Is it a homework assignment "vocabulary list," from which your child is to write sentences using those words? Is it the "allergy list" of your child's best friend, sent by her parents because she's staying for dinner?

In other words, understanding the purpose and function of the list, and knowing what to do with it—Go to the store and buy these items? Use them in cooking? Leave the list on the table?—depends on an accurate understanding of the list's genre, of what kind of list it is. When we don't know the genre, it leaves us unable to discern even how to begin to interpret any communication. Similarly, reading biblical texts requires identifying their genres, placing each passage into its correct interpretive frameworks, to understand its message accurately.

GENRE RECOGNITION USUALLY OPERATES SUBCONSCIOUSLY

Recognition of genres is something that occurs naturally and subconsciously through repeated exposure. Our life experiences and teachings make us familiar with them. When we turn on the television and see a couple of people seated behind a desk, reading sheets of paper, with a screen behind them showing pictures or a map, we automatically recognize, even without hearing what they are saying, that this is a news broadcast. We don't have to work to identify the genre, nor do we consciously think, "Okay, this is a newscast, so how do I understand it properly?" Our repeated exposure to the genre allows us to shift instantaneously into the mental interpretative framework of filtering this through the genre of a newscast.

Most of us do not have the automatic familiarity with biblical genres that subconsciously produces the proper framework through which to read them, as we do with modern genres. Thus we have to acquaint ourselves with the characteristics of biblical genres, learning how they work and how to interpret them according to their various "rules." Even with those genres that we're familiar with, we can't automatically assume a given biblical genre is identical to a similar contemporary genre.

We can take the broad biblical genre of "prophetic" literature as an example. If we assume biblical prophecy consists solely or primarily of predicting future events, that presuppositional lens ends up distorting our interpretation of prophetic passages, since only about 25 percent of Old Testament prophecy is predictive. The other 75 percent involves the divine critique of the prophets' contemporary situations, often accusing the people of specific covenant violations, calling them to repent, advising them of God's own working, and reminding them of God's instruction in how to live as God's people. If we would hope to understand them, we need to familiarize ourselves with the characteristics and purposes of this and other biblical genres that are not part of our contemporary context.

GENRES ARE CULTURALLY DEPENDENT

Even though similar genres occur within different cultures, there will be cultural differences. In reading the Bible we can't automatically assume, since we have the same broad genres today (narratives, poems, letters, etc.), that our way of reading and understanding a genre is the same as it was within the cultures of the biblical world.

For example, the major characteristics of Hebrew poetry are different from those of modern Western poetry. We expect the words at the end of lines to rhyme, or for the poems to have a regular, metrical beat. Both are rare in Hebrew poetry. Moreover, the key defining characteristic of Hebrew poetry, "parallelism"—the expression of an idea or an image through a paired couplet of lines—is quite foreign to our cultural way of writing poetry. Thus we need to familiarize ourselves with the basic qualities of parallelism, with its look and "feel," if we hope to interpret Hebrew poetry accurately and well.

Another example is the biblical genre "epistle." Although we still write letters, the constituting elements of ours differ from the first century A.D. Greco-Roman pattern—normally, an opening salutation, a prayer of thanksgiving, the body of the letter, an exhortation, and one or more closing elements. To read the New Testament Epistles effectively, we need to be aware of how the writing of letters then differed from ours today.

GENRES HAVE A "SHELF LIFE"

As times change, communication also results in the rise of new genres. One example is e-mail, a whole set of genres which did not exist thirty years ago. A genre that did not exist a hundred and fifty years ago is the telephone book. Technological advances were the catalysts that gave rise to both these genres. Other new genres develop because of cultural preferences. For example, the "reality show" is a relatively new genre of television programming.

Conversely, some genres fall into disuse, becoming dead genres; remember (if you can!) the old television variety show, or the cowboy/western drama. In written poetry, the sonnet was a beautiful and respected medium famously employed by William Shakespeare, Elizabeth Browning, and others. Except, perhaps, for a high school or college literature course, when was the last time you read a sonnet?

The relevance, here, is that we no longer use some of the biblical genres, either. Whether a similar modern genre is now different from its corresponding biblical genre (poetry, epistles), or a biblical genre is no longer part of our cultural repertoire of genres, we are "genre illiterate." For example, apocalyptic literature is not a genre we either read or write. Yet when Daniel and Revelation were composed, they were but a small part of an "apocalyptic" genre prevalent within their cultural context. Since they belong to a genre that is dead to us (outside these two books themselves), we must familiarize ourselves with the genre—its form, content, function, and life-setting—if we hope to interpret these books correctly.

Another biblical genre that has faded from our cultural use is the "proverb." To us, proverbs are nice, cute, archaic statements, but they certainly don't govern how we make decisions, nor do we use them to explain what happens in our lives. Because of our lack of familiarity with that genre, we may misinterpret biblical proverbs as we seek to apply their teaching to our lives.

For example, many biblical proverbs consist of a first line which is an exhortation to do a certain behavior. This is followed in the second line with the statement of result or consequence if that action is carried out. The first line of Proverbs 22:6 gives the command, "Train children in the right way." This is followed by the result statement in the second line, "and when old, they will not stray" (NRSV). But it runs contrary to the genre to read those consequence statements of the proverbs as assured promises. Rather, they are expressions of generalized truth. So Proverbs 22:6 is not a divine promise that if parented correctly, children will follow in the way of the Lord all their lives, or that spiritually wayward children will return to the Lord because of their spiritual upbringing. Rather, like all proverbs, it expresses a general principle that in most cases this does occur, but it's not an absolute or universal assurance.

PROSE AND POETRY

Within the Bible, the broadest literary distinction is between prose and poetry. Many translations exhibit an external formatting difference: prose is written in full sentence form in paragraphs, whereas poetry is formatted as short poetic lines. This formatting difference was not a feature of the earliest Hebrew and Greek manuscripts; still, it reflects faithfully the essential difference, and it's extremely helpful to use a translation that formats prose and poetry this way.

Besides recognizing the formal characteristics of biblical poetry, such as parallelism, we read poetry differently than prose. Prose is designed primarily to be descriptive as it gives, e.g., a sequential account of events, or an ordered discourse. Poetry, through the more frequent use of figures of speech, is designed to be more emotive, e.g., recreating the feeling of what transpired, or evoking passion as an aid to thought and decision.

The difference can be illustrated through the analogy of different genres in painting. What an artist attempts to create in a realistic painting (analogous here to prose narrative) is quite different from the intention for an impressionistic or an abstract painting (analogous to poetry). The former is designed to re-create a scene according to what it looked like, while the latter seeks to re-create the feeling(s) and mood(s) evoked by the scene or event. Thus, we read the poetry of the Psalms differently than we read the prose of the historical narratives of the Old Testament, the New Testament Gospels, and the Epistles.

FURTHER GENRE DIVISIONS WITHIN THE BIBLE

THE "BIG SEVEN"

Beyond the broad prose/poetry distinction, biblical texts can be assigned to seven main genres. Broadly speaking, there are three prose genres. First is narrative or story, comprising the bulk of Genesis through Esther, and Matthew through Acts. (When you see "story," don't think "fiction"; most stories relate events that really happened.) Second is law, or "instruction," mainly found in Exodus through Deuteronomy. The third prose genre is "epistle" or "letter," comprising Romans through Jude in the New Testament. The fourth genre is "apocalypse," Daniel 7–12 and a few other sections in the Old Testament, and Revelation in the New Testament.

The poetry division includes the fifth genre, poems or psalms— Psalms, Lamentations, and Song of Songs—and the sixth, "wisdom literature"—Proverbs, Job, and Ecclesiastes. The seventh genre, "prophecy," includes Isaiah, Jeremiah, Ezekiel, and Hosea through Malachi; it comprises poetic messages, as well as prose narratives and speeches. All these books are in the Old Testament, though the New Testament also includes short examples of each of these genres.

FURTHER GENRES/FORMS WITHIN THE BIBLE

Each of these seven genres can be subdivided further into more specific types, sometimes referred to as "forms." Just as we have many forms of stories (e.g., history writing, romance, mystery, fables, fairy tales), so too there are different types of biblical narratives, such as historical narratives, gospels, parables, etc. Those, in turn, can incorporate a whole variety of even shorter forms; examples include miracle stories, battle reports, annals, journey stories, genealogies, dream reports, and annunciation accounts.

Today, we have a variety of letters that serve different functions, e.g., business letters, junk mail, love letters. The New Testament books can also be divided based on their styles and purposes: pastoral letters such as 1 and 2 Timothy that address pastorally particular situations within a congregation or a person's life; tractate letters of a more general theological exposition, such as Romans; and sermon letters, such as Hebrews, that read like the transcript of a sermon.

The genres of modern poetry (epic poem, ode, sonnet, limerick, haiku) exhibit varying elements with which we need to be familiar if we are to properly appreciate any given poem. So, too, the psalms can be subdivided into psalms of thanksgiving (thanks to God for responding to one's petitions); hymns (praise to God for who he is and what he has done); creation psalms (praise to God as Creator); psalms of confidence (declarations of trust in God in the midst of adversity); lament psalms (cries to God in the midst of distress); Torah psalms (praise to God for his law); Royal Yahweh psalms (praise to God as king); and Royal David psalms (songs about the human ruler from the line of David). A few psalms are in other genres/forms.

Wisdom literature can be divided into traditional wisdom literature, the literary form of which is the proverb (much of the book of Proverbs), and reflective wisdom literature, whose literary style is that of a discourse reflecting on the experiences and anomalies of life (Job and Ecclesiastes).

Prophecy also includes a variety of more specific forms: e.g., oracles of disaster, woe oracles, covenant lawsuit oracles (all three highlighting the people's sins and the divinely intended, impending judgment); calls to repentance; oracles of deliverance (affirming that God will intervene to deliver his people from, or after, disaster); vision reports; reports of sign-actions (nonverbal, enacted prophecies); and call narratives (recounting God's call to prophetic ministry).

WHERE TO GO FROM HERE

The descriptions of specific biblical genres and forms could go on and on. However, the point of this chapter is to alert the reader to the importance of understanding and applying the knowledge of genre to reading the Bible, with the goal of interpreting it correctly. Just as genre is one of the blocks necessary for building communication today, so too God revealed his Word through genres that were part of ancient cultures, and understandable to the people of those times. It's not for God to reinvent the Word already revealed, but for us to work to discover its treasure, held in vessels we call "genres."

ACTION/REFLECTION SUGGESTIONS

1. Make a list of genres—choose either television or the written word—you have watched or read recently (mystery, science fiction, weather report, etc.). Think about how they differ from one another and how one particular genre, in contrast to another, affects our expectations and interpretations of what we see and read. Then reflect on how those differences in approaching contemporary genres should inform us in approaching the various genres of the Bible.

2. Read an introductory book on biblical genre, such as Gordon Fee and Douglas Stuart, *How to Read the Bible for All Its Worth*. While reading, keep a list of the new insights you gain from studying about the various genres.

3. Read the narrative account in Judges 4 about Israel's defeat of Sisera, noting features of the prose rendition (historically relevant detail, straightforward description, etc.). Then read the poetic description of the same event in Judges 5. Note the differences in the literary techniques, styles, and emphases used to describe the same event in the two different genres. Reflect on how these differences in literary presentation might inform us of how we should read other narrative and poetic passages in the Bible.

FOR FURTHER READING

Fee, Gordon, and Douglas Stuart. *How to Read the Bible for All Its Worth: A Guide to Understanding the Bible* (2nd edition). Grand Rapids: Zondervan, 1993.

I highly recommend this book as one of the first for beginning to understand the issues related to the interpretation of Scripture. It's easy to understand, yet covers the material superbly.

Griedanus, Sidney. *The Modern Preacher and the Ancient Text: Interpreting and Preaching Biblical Literature.* Grand Rapids: Eerdmans, 1988.

More advanced and technical than Fee and Stuart, because it's designed for seminary-level readers. It extensively covers the genres of Old Testament narrative and prophetic literature, and the New Testament Gospels and Epistles. It's very helpful in moving from the biblical text to the modern proclamation of that text.

Klein, George L., ed. *Reclaiming the Prophetic Mantle: Preaching the Old Testament Faithfully.* Nashville: Broadman, 1992.

For genre study, the first section of this multi-author work is very helpful, as it covers all the major Old Testament genres of narrative, law, poetry, prophets, and wisdom. Its purpose, as the title indicates, is not only to help readers understand the original genres, but to move us from the text into contemporary application.

Ryken, Leland. *Words of Delight: A Literary Introduction to the Bible* (2nd edition). Grand Rapids: Baker, 1992.

This is an excellent book that approaches the interpretation of the Bible from the standpoint of reading it appropriately as literature.

This includes not just understanding genre, but seeing how various literary techniques help us get to the message of the text. Covering both the Old and the New Testaments, this book will be of help to lay and student readers, as well as to clergy.

NOTES

1. Darby Conley, *Get Fuzzy*, http://comics.com/get_fuzzy/2003-02-14/, accessed February 4, 2009.

CULTURE

❖

Joseph Coleson

We have this treasure in jars of clay.
—2 Corinthians 4:7a

All doctrine is formulated within a cultural context.
—Thomas A. Noble

Cultures matter. Cultures matter for understanding people, and for getting along with people. In the West, if John needs to jump right into the purpose of his visit, he can apologize for his haste, do it, and be on his way. Usually, it won't matter if he's polite about it. In the East, including the Middle East, it would matter a lot. Even God didn't jump right into the business he had come for; Abraham and Sarah fixed a whole meal for the three visitors first, taking several hours, before God was "allowed" to state his business (Gen. 18:1–9).

In most of Western culture, grown women are beholden to no one for their public movements. Objection by a husband or boyfriend might even be considered a sign of an abusive relationship. Some Middle Eastern societies are similar at this point. In others, a woman seen talking in public with a man not related to her brings shame on her family. She could die at the hands of close male relatives to remove the shame. Cultures matter!

Think for a moment about things common in biblical times that we seldom or never experience: grinding grain and baking bread every day; oil lamps and cooking fires as the only evening light; oxen plowing fields and pulling wagons; sheep and goats providing milk, cheese, and meat; eating meat only on special occasions; owning one wrap-around cloak; teenage marriage; children dying in infancy; walking or riding a donkey everywhere one goes; seldom leaving one's town or village; being able to read a little, but having nothing interesting or informative to read; raisins, dried figs, and honey as almost the only sweets—our list could be nearly endless, along with our possibilities for misunderstanding their cultures.

Think for a moment about things we take for granted that no earlier cultures could have imagined: light bulbs; kitchen ranges with ovens; refrigerators; microwaves; central heating and cooling; radio; television; cell phones; computers—all these and more because of electricity and/or natural gas. Think of cars, trucks, and motorcycles; paved roads and superhighways; all retail outlets larger than a tiny room; churches; skyscrapers; railroads; airplanes; hundreds of cities larger than a few thousand people; instant world-wide communication; the Web, e-mail, blogging and personal websites; dating; organized sports; thousands of vocational choices; space travel; scuba diving; inoculations; organ transplants; frozen foods; restaurants; every person one meets being free-born. This list, too, could be endless, along with the dangers of imposing our images, assumptions, and values on their world, even if only sub-consciously.

Our purpose in this chapter is not to describe or explain the cultures reflected in the biblical record. That would require libraries, not pages. Rather, we will note examples across several areas where an accurate cultural understanding illumines a given biblical situation, event, or saying, and/or where an inaccurate understanding could be harmful. Our hope is to persuade the reader that cultural considerations are always significant and helpful in biblical study.

AN IMPORTANT ORIENTING PRINCIPLE

One important, orienting principle (or caveat) applies to our entire discussion. What the Bible describes is not always what the Bible prescribes. For example, the Bible describes wealthy and powerful men indulging in polygamy. However, if we read the Bible competently, it is clear from Genesis 1 to Revelation 22 that one man and one woman together in marriage is God's ideal, primarily because each one is always more than sufficient for the other one.

Because of the progressive nature of revelation (see chapter 10 in this work), we may take this a step further. Often, what God prescribed for ancient Israel is not what God prescribes or expects for the believer today. Moral and ethical principles are constant and enduring; moral and ethical practices often differ among cultures, and may change within a society over time. For example, idolatry, murder, adultery, and theft always are wrong. However, as Jesus taught in the Sermon on the Mount (Matt. 5–7), the heart betrays its sinfulness in thought and word, by a look and an attitude, long before the deed is done. It's these and their appearances, sounds, and textures that often vary from culture to culture.

FAMILY

Family is the context in which everyone first experiences and begins to learn about culture. In most Western societies, the nuclear family is paramount—a marriage of one man and one woman, and the children (if they produce any). Other relatives are much less important. In recent decades, more and more adults even live as singles, with or without children.

Through most of history and in much of the world today, the extended family was and is the primary social unit. In biblical times, adult sons, even married and with children, usually lived with their father's family and under his authority until his death.

Let us be clear, however, that God does not condone patriarchalism. God's early instruction was for a man to abandon his parents and cleave to his wife (Gen. 2:24). This is a strong indictment—both these verbs are very vigorous—of the usual patriarchal practice of a bride coming to live with her husband's extended family, under the authority of her husband and his parents. The biblical record of family life shows most in the ancient world never grasped this principle of Genesis 2:24, but never doubt it was God's ideal.

The importance of extended family explains why Isaac and Jacob both married cousins (Gen. 24:4, 24, 27; 29:10–28), a choice sometimes seen as ideal in that region even today. It was almost the routine for Egyptian pharaohs to marry their sisters; other ancient stories of sibling marriage survive as well. This does not mean sibling marriage was common, or even permitted, everywhere; it wasn't. But our predictable question from Genesis 4:17—Did Cain marry his sister?—would have been of little interest in antiquity.

Extended family ties explain the law of the kinsman-redeemer (Lev. 25:23–34, 47–55, *passim*). Property and persons sold because of debt were to be redeemed, so no Israelite family would be consigned to perpetual poverty. Two vivid examples are Boaz's redemption of Naomi's field (Ruth 4:1–12), and Jeremiah's redemption of his cousin's field (Jer. 32:6–15). Since Jesus came to redeem us, Jew and Gentile alike (see, e.g., Rev. 5:8–14), one conclusion must be that the triune God regards believers as family members, redeemed from the poverty of sin and death, and restored to family fellowship—sons and daughters, brothers and sisters together.

Conceptually, we understand biblical references to nursing mothers (e.g., Ex. 2:7–9; 1 Kings 3:21), to Zion/Jerusalem personified as a nursing mother (Isa. 66:7–13), and even to God by the title *Shaddai* (see ch. 12). However, the urgency is lost on us; we have forgotten that mother's milk was life, and the child deprived of milk died within days.

CLOTHING

In biblical times, the wealthy could possess a splendid wardrobe; think of Joseph's coat (Gen. 37:3). Even the average person might have a change of clothing (Ruth 3:3). But the truly poor owned a single, outer garment, which served as cloak by day and blanket by night. This is why a cloak taken as collateral for a debt was to be returned to its owner each night (Ex. 22:26–27). That every man wore such an outer garment also explains the expression "spread [one's] cloak over" a woman (Ruth 3:9; Ezek. 16:8) as a euphemism for marriage.

Public nakedness was extremely shameful in the ancient world. The prophets often threatened wayward Israel and Judah with being driven naked into exile as judgment upon their apostasy (Ezek. 16:37; Hos. 2:3). Jesus was stripped, then mocked (Matt. 27:28), and crucified naked (Luke 23:34), a humiliation so great in the Jewish culture of that day that it's not an exaggeration to say Jesus experienced, publicly, the shame of sexual abuse.

Purple clothing was the color of royalty and/or great wealth, because purple dye came exclusively from boiling the *murex*, several species of mollusks found only along the Phoenician coast. Wherever "purple" is mentioned in Scripture, it signifies wealth and privilege.

DWELLINGS

Most homes were of stone, or stone courses in the lower portions of the walls, and adobe-type mud-brick courses in the upper portions. Remains of stone staircases in many excavations show that houses often had two stories in the more prosperous periods of Israel's history, and into New Testament times. The typical Israelite house fronted on the street. One entered a central courtyard open to the sky, flanked by a roofed storage room on one side and a roofed room where the animals were sheltered at night on the other side. The courtyard usually had a covered opening to a hewn-out cistern below, a fire pit, and perhaps an oven. Beyond these parallel "rooms" in a single-story house was a sleeping room the length of these three and perpendicular to them. The roof usually was flat, and some household activities occurred there—for example, drying flax (Josh. 2:6) and grain, and sleeping under the sky during the summer. The Torah required a parapet around the perimeter of the roof to prevent falls (Deut. 22:8).

By our standards, ancient houses were tiny. The "governor's house" in Old Testament Beersheba is no larger than two rooms together in many North American houses today. Even the powerful King Ahab's winter palace in Jezreel (1 Kings 21:1) was no larger than the average middle-class house built in every American city and town since the 1970s.

FARMING, FOOD, AND WATER

Most Israelites were subsistence farmers during the whole of the Old Testament period(s), growing or raising almost everything they needed. Most fields, orchards, and vineyards we would measure in acres, not in tens of acres, because they could neither plant, harvest, nor store the produce of more land than that. Most acreage was terraced with stones, both to clear the stones from the ground, and to slow the erosion of the hill slopes that constituted most of the arable land in Israel's heartland, the central hill country.

Wheat, barley, olives (for oil), grapes (for wine and raisins), figs, and pomegranates were primary crops. The ideal was for each farmer to live securely in his own house, "under his own vine and under his own fig tree" (1 Kings 4:25, author's translation). Cucumbers, lentils, beans, onions, leaks, and garlic were common vegetables. Cheese, curds, and milk came from goats and sheep more than from cows. The average Israelite ate meat only on special occasions; mutton, lamb, and goat were most common, though royalty and the wealthy ate meat more often and could afford to include beef and game animals in their daily fare (1 Kings 4:22–23).

Streams don't flow year-round in the Israelite and Judean hill country. When Israel entered the land under Joshua, cities and towns were located only near a flowing spring or a dug well. The invention of waterproof plaster made from lime allowed for hundreds of brand-new settlements in early Israel, as cisterns now could be dug into the porous limestone bedrock, and sealed against leakage. Rain supplied water for the field crops; trees and vines survived through the rainless summer; garden vegetables, drinking water for humans and animals, and other household water needs, were all supplied when the cisterns filled in the rainy winter season. We could discuss hundreds of references, but among the most poignant is Jeremiah 2:13, "For two disastrous things my people have done: Me, they have forsaken—a well of living water, and they have carved out for themselves cisterns, broken cisterns, which cannot hold water" (author's translation).

PASTORAL NOMADISM

Abraham and Sarah, Isaac and Rebekah, and Jacob and his family all lived as pastoral nomads. That is, they depended mostly on flocks of sheep and goats, and moved in seasonally predictable patterns to find grazing and water for them. They usually lived in tents, though for a time Isaac and Rebekah lived in a house in the town of Gerar (Gen. 26:6–8). These rich "sheiks" possessed many flocks and, therefore, had many servants and hired men. Abraham, for example, fielded a small army to rescue his nephew Lot (Gen. 14:14). This armed readiness, mobility, and the fact that pastoralists moved through the territory of the settled farmers twice a year in the hill country of ancient Israel, made them a continuing threat to the settled farmers.

Pastoralists carry all their possessions with them when they move, which they usually do several times each year. This means, of course, their possessions are limited to the basics. Sometimes they can harvest a crop of grain (Gen. 26:12), but usually they have to buy or trade for the wheat or barley with which to make their daily bread.

Most Israelites were not pastoralists once Israel began to settle the land under Joshua (but see Jer. 35). But Israel remembered its ancestors and almost every household had a few sheep and goats. References to pastoral life and to these animals permeate the Scriptures, both the Old and New Testaments.

CITIES AND TOWNS

Ancient cities were tiny by our standards. Grandiose as Nebuchadnezzar's ambitious building projects made it, Babylon was only a little larger than three square miles; Babylon (first) and Nineveh (second) were by far the largest cities of ancient western Asia. Amazingly, David's Jerusalem was only about thirteen acres in size, with a population of about fifteen hundred.

Towns as small as five or six acres usually had defensive walls. The population of a town that size would have been between seven hundred and nine hundred people. Unwalled villages could be as few as fifty people; their houses were often arranged in a semicircle to nearly a full circle, with the houses' outer, back walls providing a limited defensive perimeter. When danger threatened, villagers usually fled to the nearby walled "city" for refuge.

With the invention of cisterns, villages could exist wherever relatively good soil and pastureland could be found. A city or town (the Hebrew word is the same) needed a defensible position, usually a slight prominence or a real hilltop. Stone defensive walls were built to take advantage of the hill's terrain. Gates required special fortification, as attacks were concentrated on burning or breaking them down. The most important towns were seaports, and towns located at the junction of two (or more) roads.

The number of large cities had grown considerably by New Testament times. Rome, capital of the Empire, was not much larger than Babylon had been, but its population was more densely packed, numbering more than a million. During Paul's stay, Ephesus is estimated to have been the fourth largest city in the world, with a population of about 250,000. Its theater (Acts 19:31) held about 24,000. Jerusalem was much larger than in David's day, but was a small city by Roman standards; its normal population usually is estimated at about 30,000.

TRADE AND TRAVEL

The most important international trade route in antiquity ran from Egypt to Mesopotamia, not many miles from Jerusalem and through Israelite territory for about one hundred miles of its length. A second important route ran through Israelite territory east of the Jordan. In Old Testament times, much of Israel's prosperity derived from international trade along these two routes. Of course, it also cut the other way; armies of conquest coming along these routes subjected Israel and Judah to one empire after another, from Assyria's zenith to Rome's.

The scope and abundance of international trade increased in the later monarchy. Ezekiel 27:17 lists wheat, honey, oil, and balm as the agricultural products Judah and Israel traded to the world through Tyre, in exchange for luxury goods from many other lands. The average farmer, though making possible the exports, did not benefit from the imports. Amos and Micah, especially, called out the rich, including the women of leading families, for indulging themselves in imported luxury goods at the expense of the poor (Amos 2:6; 3:15; 4:1–3; Mic. 2:1–2; 3:1–4).

JUSTICE AND GOVERNMENT

Throughout Israel's history, justice was dispensed by the elders in the city gate, along with other legal transactions (Deut. 16:18–20; Ruth 4:1–12). In the period of the judges, appeal was to the current judge or leader (Judg. 4:5). Later, the king was the court of appeals; when David shirked this duty late in his reign, his son Absalom took advantage of the situation, judged cleverly and perhaps even justly, and won the hearts of many of the people (2 Sam. 15:1–6).

Life for the average Israelite under Solomon and the later kings did not change much, except in a few respects. Central governments always collect taxes. The Israelite farmer paid a tax in wheat, in wine, and in olive oil. In addition, some subjects were liable to a "labor tax," having to work on the king's building projects one or two months a year. When kings and their courts became corrupt, the small farmer often suffered. More than one of the prophets accused the rich and powerful of unjustly seizing the lands of those who had fallen into debt, and evicting them to build large estates (Amos 3:15; 5:11–12; Mic. 2:2, 9). The lucky among the poor then became servants on the land they formerly had owned.

MATTERS OF FAITH

Culture includes faith and religious expression. The Torah (Pentateuch) instructed Israel to offer God the firstborn of their domestic animals and the first-ripe of their major crops each year. Sacrifices were prescribed and/or accepted on numerous occasions. Worship included the singing represented by the psalms, songs, and prayers for all occasions: joy and thanksgiving, remembrance, lament, worry, repentance, and other concerns. Though normally only adult males were required to be present (Ex. 23:17), all—men, women, and children—were allowed and encouraged to be present in worship gatherings (Ex. 15:1–21; 1 Sam. 1:1—2:11; Neh. 8:3).

A FINAL THOUGHT

Of course, we have only begun to scratch the surface in this short chapter. We could illustrate the range of biblical culture and cultures by talking about birth, love, marriage, death, burial, education, music, games, cosmetics, household furnishings and utensils, and other occupations—our list could go on and on. Truly, every verse of the Bible reflects culture, both explicitly and implicitly at the same time.

Please remember, though, two other important, demonstrable principles as you begin or continue your own lifetime of study in the Bible and the cultures represented or mentioned in it. First, culture is of God, because God created us for relationship and culture is relationship. Second, all cultures (including our own) stand in need of correction and redemption, because our first parents, and we after them, thought we could do relationship better than God. One of the tasks of ministry is to speak redemptive truth in love to ours and other cultures, as God gives us cultural wisdom and opportunity.

REFLECTION/ACTION SUGGESTIONS

1. Read and ponder the examples of best and not-so-great practices reported in part 3 of this book, A Wesleyan Approach to Interpreting Scripture. Consider each as a guide to better Bible study habits and, ultimately, to better Christian practice for yourself and those you lead.

2. Make a conscious habit of asking cultural questions of every passage and verse of Scripture. For every public presentation or leadership role in a study session, research at least one cultural highlight or insight to share with the congregation or study group.

3. In your ministry settings, ask: What is or are the culture(s) of this place, this group, this congregation? What cultural insights will help me minister to them and better equip them for ministry? What cultural norms or practices need strengthening? Which need changing or redeeming? What have we learned about, and from, biblical culture(s) that could be helpful in our ministry setting(s)?

FOR FURTHER READING

A good Bible dictionary.

The single most important reference for learning about biblical culture and cultures is an adequate, up-to-date Bible dictionary. The most comprehensive is the six-volume *Anchor Bible Dictionary*, published by Doubleday (Random House). Two other good ones (one volume each) are *Harper's Bible Dictionary*, published by Harper & Row (a bit on the liberal side in some of its articles), and *Holman Bible Dictionary*, published by Holman Bible Publishers (a bit on the conservative side in some of its articles).

Hareuveni, Nogah. *Nature in Our Biblical Heritage* (1980); *Tree and Shrub in Our Biblical Heritage* (1984); *Desert and Shepherd in Our Biblical Heritage* (1991). Kiryat Ono, Israel: Neot Kedumim Ltd.

A wonderful three-volume series by a *sabra* (native Israeli), a practicing naturalist privileged to grow up in Israel in a family of naturalists.

In the subjects Hareuveni discusses, your knowledge will be increased and your understanding illuminated by these volumes as by nothing else except, perhaps, your own extended sojourn in the biblical lands themselves.

King, Philip J., and Lawrence E. Stager. *Life in Biblical Israel.* Louisville: Westminster John Knox Press, 2001.

The best, most comprehensive, most up-to-date, one-volume resource on life in ancient Israel. A bonus is the 228 illustrations throughout the volume, mostly color photographs, but including also maps, plans, and other line drawings.

Wight, Fred H. *Manners and Customs of Bible Lands.* Chicago: Moody Press, 1953.

An old but still interesting standby, available from used-book sellers, in-store, and online.

FIGURATIVE LANGUAGE

Elaine Bernius

Your word is a lamp to my feet and a light for my path.
—Psalm 119:105

The metaphor is probably the most fertile power possessed by man.
—José Ortega y Gasset

After a fun-filled morning at preschool, my four-year-old son bursts through the back door and exclaims, "Wow, Mom. I'm starving!" As the receiver of this communication, I now have a choice to make concerning my response. I can calmly begin putting some peanut butter on crackers while gently reminding him to wash his hands; I can acknowledge his statement, but let him know lunch won't be served for another hour; or I can lay him down and begin spoon-feeding him broth while frantically dialing 9-1-1. The disparity among these potential responses is based upon my possible interpretations of the language he used.

There are two broad categories of language: literal language and figurative language. Both types can communicate meaning and express truth. However, literal language is meant to be taken at face value, holding to the strictest sense of meaning, while figurative language takes us beyond the meaning of the words themselves, painting and bringing to life mental images for the receiver.

In the example above, instead of stating literally "I'm hungry," my son chose to communicate using figurative language. My mistake—if I had called 9-1-1—would have been in my failure to recognize figurative language, resulting in a literal interpretation of a figurative statement. This misunderstanding would have produced a ridiculous outcome.

Biblical language contains the same broad categories—literal and figurative—as our daily language. As this example shows, it's vital for us to be able to recognize the presence of figurative language and interpret accordingly. The correspondence is simple. If the biblical author is using literal language, I should interpret literally. If the biblical author is using figurative language, I should interpret figuratively. My interpretation approach can be determined only in response to the language received. I cannot decide beforehand to be a literal interpreter or a figurative interpreter. Rather, I should say that "I take the Bible's words the way they were meant to be taken— either literally or figuratively."

RECOGNIZING AND IDENTIFYING FIGURATIVE LANGUAGE

How do we recognize figurative language so that we know to interpret figuratively rather than literally? A huge range of figurative language is available in every human language. Some figures of speech are simple and apparent, while others are complex.

The authors of the Bible did utilize, it's true, some Hebrew and Greek forms of figurative language that will be difficult for us to recognize.

However, a great number of biblical figures of speech are common in English as well. For example, the simile is a simple comparison; it's very common in English and is also used in many beloved biblical passages, such as, "The kingdom of heaven is like a mustard seed" (Matt. 13:31).

Familiarizing myself with the range of figures of speech available in English will make biblical figurative language much more accessible. This step will be ongoing. The more I sensitize myself to recognizing figurative language, the more figurative language I will be able to recognize!

Some of the most common biblical figures of speech include simile, metaphor, contrast, hyperbole, synecdoche, wordplay, irony, and personification. To this list we could add euphemism, metonymy, hendiadys, symbol, apostrophe, onomatopoeia, and allusion, not to mention poetic techniques such as alliteration, assonance, parallelism, inclusio, chiasm, and acrostic. The intention here is not to overwhelm, but rather to open our eyes to the incredible richness waiting to be discovered in the Bible. Are you looking for a good sermon illustration, something that can really grab people's attention and allow them to grasp a spiritual truth? Have I got the book for you!

Let's assume a scenario: You've read through a passage twice, and now are fairly certain it contains figurative language. The next step is to identify the type(s) of figurative language being used. Identifications are not ends in themselves. Our goal is not to become expert figures-of-speech-labelers. But we do this step for two reasons.

The first reason is simple: If I can label it, I confirm the presence of figurative language, thereby determining that I will be interpreting figuratively. Second, identifications allow me to understand the author's intention. If I can recognize the statement, "The fear of the Lord is a fountain of life" (Prov. 14:27), as a metaphor, then I know the author intends for me to see a similarity between these two entities. If I recognize the irony in the life of Joseph—the one sold as a slave by his brothers ultimately becomes their master and sets them free from famine— then I understand that the author intends for me to contrast the unexpected with the expected. It was because of this situational irony in his life that Joseph stated, "You intended to harm me, but God intended it for good" (Gen. 50:20). The point here is not so much to know the terminology, as it is to know what to do with figurative language when we see it.

UNCOVERING MEANING IN CONTEXT

Let's return to our opening example. Simply by recognizing the presence of figurative language and identifying his use of hyperbole, I could accurately conclude my son is not literally starving. What is he trying to tell me? He's telling me he's hungry. A basic goal of listening is accurately assessing the sender's intended meaning. To do this, the listener depends on clues from the broader situation; "context is everything" in all communication—including reading the Bible.

The author often gives us a straightforward explanation of the image used. In Genesis 22:17, for example, the Lord says, "I will . . . make your descendants as numerous as the stars in the sky." This is a basic comparison clearly highlighting a single point of similarity between two unlike objects. It's simple. Likewise, following the parable of the sower in Mark 4 (also Matt. 13; Luke 8), Jesus took the time to explain the meaning of each element of the parable. Great! No need to look further. Trying to glean more will lead me down a road the author never intended for me to travel, and will very likely get me into interpretive trouble. Other examples of this occur in Isaiah 5:1–7 and Matthew 13:36–43.

In other cases, authorial interpretations are lacking, but the meaning becomes clear in the larger context. For example, 2 Samuel 12 begins with a parable spoken by the prophet Nathan. The identifications of the characters within this story can be understood only in light of the preceding narrative involving Uriah, Bathsheba, and David. Similarly, without an understanding of the full account of Jesus' trial before Pilate, one would never grasp the irony in his multiple declarations of Jesus as "king" in John 19.

Other passages illuminate the author's intent by using parallel images. For example, Luke 15 contains three parables about a losing and a finding. Obviously, Jesus was teaching to a theme here. Therefore, I must be careful to avoid an interpretation of one figure that is inconsistent with the other two. (For other examples, see Matt. 5:13–16; 13:44–46; Job 27:18; 29:6; Ps. 133.)

Finally, there are instances in which the context of a figurative image does very little to shed light on its meaning. In some of these cases, the image is not explained because the meaning would have been straightforward to the original audience, but it's lost on us due to our differing cultural context.

Take, for example, Psalm 133 in which the pleasantness of brotherly unity is compared with the pleasantness of oil running down Aaron's head and beard. That doesn't sound so pleasant to me! Don't just walk away from a perplexing image such as this, though. Take the time to seek out a reliable Bible dictionary or commentary to explain the image. If you do, you will discover that oil was used to clean and refresh the body; therefore, its imagery would have elicited thoughts of restoration and soothing. Discovering that, the pleasantness of the image becomes much more understandable. Going a step further, the connection of the oil with Aaron indicates his anointing as high priest, a position whose primary function was to bring unity between God and man. Indeed, how good and pleasant it is! (Similar examples include Song 4:1 and Prov. 11:22.)

Other images not illuminated by their contexts can prove not only perplexing, but extremely difficult and disturbing. Consider

2 Corinthians 11:8, in which the apostle Paul claims he "stole" from the churches he served. Is it possible the early church overlooked such a blatant transgression? Or when God is said to "hate" Esau (Mal. 1:2–3; Rom. 9:13) and when Jesus tells us to "hate" our parents (Luke 14:26), we are left reeling in shock. How can these statements exist within the larger context of Scripture which teaches that God is love and which commands us to honor our parents? Am I to believe statements which seem so unreasonable, so incomprehensible?

While there is nothing in the immediate context of either of these examples to explain the use of figurative language, an understanding of the figure of speech known as hyperbole quickly alerts us to the appeal for "shock value" in the excessive exaggeration of these statements. With this knowledge, I avoid being drawn into an interpretation that would be unreasonable in light of the whole of Scripture and Christian witness concerning these passages.

Allow me to give one caution. As we begin to recognize and understand figurative language, we often are tempted to take images too far. For example, in the parable of the prodigal son, it's fairly clear whom the father and the brothers are representing. The temptation then arises to assign representative meaning to other components of the story, such as the pigs the younger brother feeds, or the ring the father gives. These are simply narrative elements that supplement the story. Don't feel a need to assign symbolic meaning to every detail or to play out every image to its fullest extent.

This caution should be heeded particularly when exploring figurative language that tells us about God. Psalm 113:5 asks, "Who is like the Lord our God?" The answer—no one. So to describe God, the Bible compares God to things or people we do understand or know. God is described with images of a loving father and a comforting mother (Ps. 103:13; Isa. 66:13); a sovereign king and a humble servant (Matt. 21:1–11; Rev. 19:16; Isa. 52:13—53:12; John 13:5–17); a mighty warrior and a capable midwife (Ps. 68; 22:9–10); a terrifying thunderstorm and a spoken word (Nah. 1:3; Ps. 29; John 1:1–14); and a treasured friend and a gentle shepherd (John 15:13–15; Ps. 23; Matt. 18:12–14; John 10:11; Heb. 13:20).

The simple fact that we have all of these (and many more!) images to describe God is because it's impossible to learn everything there is to learn about God from one image. God is unlike any one person or thing. Therefore, we can't expect any single figure of speech to be able to contain God. None of them is perfect or complete. Each figure points to a certain aspect of God, so that all together they form a fuller picture of who God is. Avoid the temptation to take any one image too far.

GOING BEYOND MEANING

Discovering the author's intended meaning is a basic goal of communication. However, the purpose of figurative language is to take us beyond the meaning of the words themselves. Therefore, while literal language engages the hearer primarily on a cognitive level, figurative language aims to go beyond the cognitive to engage our emotions as well.

In our example, my son chose to communicate using the figurative "I'm starving!" instead of a literal equivalent such as, "Mom, I'd like some lunch." While I might cognitively process the meaning of those two statements in the same way, he chose to use figurative language because he wanted me to go beyond a cognitive awareness of his hunger. His goal was to motivate me to action; therefore, he used language that would reach my emotions.

You see, while a basic goal of communication is to discover intended meaning, its ultimate goal is to elicit a response from the receiver. When I responded by making his lunch, I was responding to his emotive appeal. If I had responded by delaying lunch, I would have failed to allow his emotional plea to motivate me to immediate action.

Of course, in our daily responses to figurative language, even when we are able to accurately assess the speaker's intended meaning, we may or may not choose to respond with the intended response. (This is especially true when dealing with a four-year-old!) However, when we are interpreting figurative language in the Bible, it should be our goal not only to respond to the intended meaning, but also to respond with the intended response.

"As far as the east is from the west, so far has he removed our transgressions from us" (Ps. 103:12). I can read this verse and understand that the Lord has taken away my sin. That is its meaning. But these words are meant to inspire me, to motivate me, to move my emotions. Can you grasp this image? I honestly cannot even wrap my thoughts around the expanse "as far as the east is from the west." It boggles my mind! To think that is how far my sins have been taken from me is overwhelming. I should be amazed by that image.

In a very real sense, if we as readers never move beyond the cognitive level (asking, "What does this image mean?"), then we have failed to receive the Lord's communication. For example, if I am not moved with compassion by the depth of Job's misery that "outweigh[s] the sand of the seas" (Job 6:3), or if my heart is not pulled taut between despair and elation as I experience the contrasts of Romans 5, then my interpretive process is ultimately unsuccessful.

If our goal is not simply to understand the intended meaning of the Bible, but also to respond with the intended response, then these emotive reactions are not merely optional. God has given us his Word as it is for a purpose, and that purpose goes beyond elucidating meaning. If mere understanding were God's solitary concern, God would not have communicated through figurative language.

Encountering the Word of God can change us to our very core if we will allow it to do so. In its pages, I can soar like an eagle or be brought low into the depths of the earth. In its poetry, mountains sing and trees clap along with us in irrepressible praise to the Lord. Through its images, we can feel the separation of God's judgment (Joel 3:12–13; Matt. 13:24–30), the might of God's throne (Isa. 6; Rev. 19), the awesomeness of God's majesty (Mark 9:2–3), and the acceptance of God's love (Hos. 1–3; Luke 15:11–32).

Don't simply reduce an image to its intended meaning. Allow the image to take root in your imagination. Allow it to carry you along and enfold you in its depths. In reality, a sensitive reader will often be grabbed by the emotion and intensity of figurative language even before its meaning is fully processed. Make that your goal.

CONNECTING WITH OUR WORLD TODAY

In many ways, figurative language is timeless. Its use in communication spans all generations and all cultures. While it might be possible for me to communicate without using any form of figurative language, it would be difficult and it certainly would not be natural. How incredible it is to see that God meets us where we are, speaking to us in the way we speak with one another!

Ultimately, the goal of the hermeneutical process is to allow us to engage with Scripture in a way that changes our lives today. In order for this to happen, you may wish at times to "repackage" a biblical image to make it more contemporary, thereby making it more tangible to modern imaginations. This could mean explaining an unfamiliar image more fully. For example, in his book *A Shepherd Looks at Psalm 23*, Phillip Keller gives insights into a pastoral setting with which we are generally unfamiliar.

Or consider Isaiah 40:31, "But those who wait on the Lord will renew their strength. They will soar on wings like eagles" (author's translation). I was recently on a theme park ride which simulated hang gliding. As I soared above trees and mountain streams, felt the thrill of flying through the clouds with the wind on my face, and marveled at the immense beauty of the pictures of creation below me, I realized this is how it feels to "soar on wings like eagles." Even though I had walked onto that ride a bit weary and faint from a busy day, I walked out feeling exhilarated and alive, yet relaxed and peaceful. Perhaps this is a way to express the sense of calm freedom that comes from waiting on the Lord.

Other repackagings could include an expression of the "land flowing with milk and honey" (Ex. 3:8, *passim*) in terms of modern representations of lushness and abundance, or casting the "great cloud of witnesses" metaphor of Hebrews 12:1 in terms of a sporting arena. Notice that these examples do not abandon the biblical imagery; they simply utilize them in a way that engages the imaginations of today's listeners. Often we try to invent a new image to fit the meaning, only to discover that it's much less precise than the original. Don't try to reinvent the wheel; just adjust its alignment if necessary.

As you see, there is flexibility to work within biblical images and, at times, even to allow an image to take you beyond the bounds of the original authorial intent. As it relates to figurative language, we see an example of this type of progressive symbolic interpretation in the Old Testament festival of the Passover. The images woven into this feast in Exodus 12 served as reminders to Israel of their salvation by God from bondage in Egypt. Jesus then reinterpreted these symbols in the Last Supper (Matt. 26; Mark 14; Luke 22) as reminders of Christ's sacrifice for our salvation from the bondage of sin. For us today, the imagery of Communion rarely brings to mind the Passover, even though the one came out of the other. While Scripture does this, such expansion of meaning on our part should always be done judiciously, measuring the words of any interpretation against the whole of Scripture, against reason, tradition, and experience. Let us never discount the power of the Holy Spirit to move and guide us within the interpretive process, always remembering that the interpretive process never exceeds the power of the Holy Spirit.

ENJOYING THE IMAGERY OF THE BIBLE

The treasure of the Word of the Lord is immense and valuable as well as incredibly beautiful. Its intricate figures of speech and beautiful imagery are glorious jewels which catch our eye and dazzle us with their brilliance. It's true that some hard work may be required as you mine these images. But in the end, not only will your heart be opened to a greater clarity of meaning, but your experience of the Word will be enriched as you respond to God with your whole being. Let the Bible come to life as its imagery captivates you in its vividness!

ACTION/REFLECTION SUGGESTIONS

1. (For this one, you may want to be alone where others cannot hear you.) Read Psalm 19 aloud, as expressively and with as much fervor as you possibly can. Go overboard with it! As you read, allow yourself to be caught up and carried along in the beautiful imagery and lilting poetry of the passage. Don't try to understand the images completely; just feel the words.

2. In order to practice recognizing and identifying figures of speech, make a photocopy of Psalm 19 and highlight all the examples of figurative language. Find as many as you can. If you aren't sure, mark it anyway. Err on the figurative side. (Astounding, isn't it?)

3. Pastors and teachers: Challenge yourself to preach or teach an upcoming sermon or lesson in which you use only biblical illustrations. Remember, you can repackage them to make them more contemporary for today's audience, but stay true to each image. Stretch yourself to help your congregation be inspired and amazed by the images of the Bible.

FOR FURTHER READING

Osborne, Grant R. *The Hermeneutical Spiral: A Comprehensive Introduction to Biblical Interpretation.* Downers Grove, Ill.: InterVarsity, 1991.

Chapter 4 in this book is a discussion of a variety of syntactical issues. For the purposes of our discussion here, this chapter is most helpful for its fairly detailed description and examples of a variety of figures of speech. If it frustrated you that I gave an entire list of figures of speech, but didn't have a chance to describe any of them, this is a great place for you to start!

Ryken, Leland, James C. Wilhoit, and Tremper Longman III, eds. *Dictionary of Biblical Imagery.* Downers Grove, Ill.: InterVarsity, 1998.

This volume serves as an excellent reference tool for gaining greater understanding and insight into biblical images. Its topical arrangement allows the reader to gain broader awareness of the use of an image throughout Scripture, as well as within any specific context.

THEOLOGY

Christopher T. Bounds

Timothy, guard what has been entrusted to your care.
Turn away from godless chatter and the opposing ideas of
what is falsely called knowledge, which some have professed
and in so doing have wandered from the faith.

—1 Timothy 6:20–21

If you desire to read the scripture . . . have a constant eye to the
analogy of faith; the connexion and harmony there is between those
grand, fundamental doctrines, Original Sin, Justification by Faith,
the New Birth, and Inward and Outward Holiness.

—John Wesley

INTRODUCTION

If you've been a part of a group Bible study, debated Scripture with friends, or listened to Jehovah's Witnesses, you've seen and heard many different interpretations of biblical teaching. Often, you recognize that the issue isn't the authority of Scripture. Most people in your discussion, if not all, accept the Bible as the final authority in all matters of faith and practice. The problem arises in how the Bible is interpreted. There appear to be as many understandings of Scripture as there are readers. Sometimes these differences are minor and can be brought together, while others simply are irreconcilable. Even more exasperating, these different readings of the biblical text aren't isolated to minor issues, but often involve doctrines at the heart of Christianity.

Let's illustrate the problem with three examples. The first addresses the issue of baptism: by whose name are people to be baptized? Most Christians have been baptized in the "name of the Father, and of the Son, and of the Holy Spirit," as Jesus instructed in Matthew 28:19. However, in the book of Acts, the early church baptized believers in the "name of Jesus Christ" (Acts 2:38; 8:16; 10:48; 19:5). Which baptismal formula is correct?

Second, can Christians be empowered presently to live in obedience to Jesus Christ? Can the power of sin be broken in human life? John clearly states, "No one who lives in him keeps on sinning," and "he cannot go on sinning, because he has been born of God" (1 John 3:6, 9). However, in an apparent testimony about his current Christian experience, Paul declared, "For I have the desire to do what is good, but I cannot carry it out. For what I do is not the good I want to do; no, the evil I do not want to do—this I keep on doing" (Rom. 7:18–19). How are we to reconcile these two seemingly disparate biblical testimonies?

Third, who is Jesus Christ? Certainly, some New Testament texts point to Christ being eternally God, along with the Father (John 1:1–2, 18). However, other passages seem to portray Christ as an exalted creature, the most elevated one in the created order, but not always God with the Father (John 14:28; Rom. 8:29; Col. 1:15). Is Jesus Christ truly and eternally God, equal to the Father, or is he a creature, a part of the created order, made in time by the Father and therefore less than God?

As we study the Bible, we are confronted inevitably with difficult texts of Scripture to understand in light of other passages. To resolve such problems and arrive at sound Christian instruction, we must employ a theological hermeneutic.

THE BIBLE IS THEOLOGICAL

To begin, most Christians rightly share with historic Christianity a basic assumption: while there is obvious diversity in Scripture, there is a recognizable unity as well. While any individual Old or New Testament book does not necessarily point to a single over-arching story that unites it with all other biblical books, as a whole they do paint a grand narrative of God and God's relationship with the created order. The Bible speaks of the triune God who created all that exists, of the fall of humanity in the garden with its disastrous impact upon the created order, of God's work of redemption through the call of Israel, the incarnation of the Son of God, the birth of the church by the Spirit, and the final consummation of God's purposes for humanity and the created order.

The Bible reveals to us a coherent picture of God, creation, sin, redemption, and consummation through its instructions, testimonies, stories, liturgies, and historical accounts. The Old and New Testaments make known a cohesive divine truth about the ultimate concerns of life, forming the foundation for Christian doctrine. As such, they are theological.

INTERPRETING THE BIBLE'S THEOLOGY

The task of Christian theology is to give a faithful account of the Bible's doctrinal teaching. To do so, it focuses on the whole of Scripture more than its individual parts. While it's concerned with the message of each book and an understanding of every passage in its literary-historical context, the center of attention is the big picture. It asks how we are to understand the major theological themes of Scripture in light of the full biblical testimony. Therefore, as we attempt to understand a particular doctrinal idea, such as the person of the Holy Spirit, our focus is not simply on Jesus' instruction found in the Upper Room Discourse (John 14–16), but also on Luke's and

Paul's discussions, as well as on any Old and New Testament writer who spoke about the Holy Spirit or hinted of him.

The priority of the whole of Scripture over the individual text is seen also in Christian theology's use of the "analogy of faith." When it approaches a thorny biblical passage that is difficult to square with other scriptural texts, it seeks to interpret that passage in the light of clearer texts and allow the "whole of Scripture" on the subject to guide the interpretation of the problematic part. For example, in regard to the question of which name is to be used in Christian baptism, Jesus' command to baptize in the Trinitarian name (Matt. 28:19), the mention of Trinitarian persons in New Testament invocations (Col. 1:3–8) and benedictions (2 Cor. 13:14), and the overall scriptural testimony to the Trinity have shaped how the baptismal accounts in the book of Acts are interpreted theologically.

Historically, Christian theology begins its work with humble recognition of the necessity of the Holy Spirit's illuminating presence, working through the body of Christ. Making sense of the whole of God's witness found in Scripture can't be done through mere human ability, nor can it be accomplished alone. The Holy Scriptures are given first and foremost to the church by God, and the Holy Spirit works within the church to lead her people into all its truth. As such, the theological enterprise is not done by individuals in isolation from the church, but by people who are actively committed to the church and work for the sake of the church.

The need for the Holy Spirit's guidance through the body of Christ can be seen in the fact that working with a theological approach is not as simple as it may appear initially. Reading the Bible theologically is not easy. There are many challenges in this interpretive work and not recognizing them can be perilous—can become a catalyst for poor, erroneous, and even heretical doctrinal readings of Scripture.

One of the bigger hurdles to be cleared is recognizing that the Bible teaches primarily in narrative forms and not in propositional statements, as we see in the synoptic accounts of Jesus' earthly life and ministry. While scriptural narratives communicate theological ideas, they're not as clear to a modern reader as developed, orderly, and logical treatments of a subject.

Also, we can detect doctrinal and ethical development in Scripture from the Old through the New Testaments, as observed in the movement from polygamy's toleration (as in the case of Jacob in Gen. 29) to monogamy's mandate (1 Cor. 7:2; 1 Tim. 3:12), and in the earliest church's slow but growing perception of the inclusion of the Gentiles in God's work of redemption (Acts 10). Thus, we can't take one particular passage of Scripture as necessarily the final word on a topic, nor even always reconcile it easily with other biblical teaching. Rather, we must see each passage within the flow of the history of God's revelation and of the Bible's inspired reflection on it.

Similarly, some biblical ideas exist only in embryonic form in the Bible, never fully developed in Scripture, requiring the church to go further than what the biblical texts state explicitly. In such cases, the church does not change biblical testimonies, but develops them to their logical end, as we see in the doctrine of the Trinity and know in our understanding of the Holy Spirit. Our belief in one God in three divine persons is never explicitly taught in the Bible, but represents a trajectory set forth there (Matt. 3:16; John 14:25—15:27; 1 Cor. 12:4–6; 1 John 3:23—4:3; Rev. 1:4–6, *passim*). Similarly, the New Testament never clearly states the Holy Spirit is a divine person, equal to the Father and the Son, but it does point to his deity (Matt. 12:31–32; Acts 5:3–4, *passim*).

WESLEYAN INTERPRETATION OF THE BIBLE'S THEOLOGY

With these basic points in mind, let's direct our attention to the Wesleyan interpretation of the Bible's theology. Specifically, the Wesleyan account of Christian doctrine is formed through prayerful dialogue and scriptural reflection within three theological communities in the larger body of Christ—historic orthodoxy, Protestantism, and the Wesleyan/Holiness Movement. Each community reads the Bible theologically, attempting to hear the whole counsel of Scripture regarding the Bible's doctrinal themes and using the "analogy of faith" to come to grips with tricky passages. Each has confronted substantively the challenges to doing theological work.

Sometimes the relationship of these interpretive traditions in the formation of Wesleyan doctrine is described as three concentric circles, with historic orthodoxy forming the center, Protestantism the subsequent ring, and Wesleyanism the outmost circle. At the center of Wesleyan doctrine is historic Christian orthodoxy, summarized in the classical statements of the Apostles' and Nicene Creeds. These creedal formulations outline Christianity's systematic account of the grand theological themes of Scripture on God, creation, fall, redemption, and consummation. They provide the theological reading of the Bible's overarching narrative. Wesleyan denominations do not always recite these creeds in worship, at times even shunning their use, yet they form the heart of the Wesleyan doctrinal construction of Scripture's theology.

The influence of the Apostles' and Nicene creeds in The Wesleyan Church's doctrinal statements is seen in two ways. First, the Articles of Religion follow their sequential order: Articles 1–4 address the Trinity (Father, Son, Holy Spirit) and creation; Articles 6–8 summarize the formation and fall of humanity; Articles 9–14 treat the doctrine of redemption; Articles 15–17 state beliefs regarding the church; Articles 18–21 discuss God's final consummative work.

Second, the bulk of the Wesleyan Articles is grounded in the orthodox teaching summarized in the creeds: belief in the one triune God (Art. 1); in creation (Art. 2); in the fall of humanity and sin (Art. 8); in the life, atoning death, and bodily resurrection of Jesus Christ (Art. 9); in the full divine and human natures of Jesus Christ (Art. 3); in the full deity of the Holy Spirit and in the agency of the Holy Spirit in creation and salvation (Art. 4); in the universal and local church (Art. 16); in the second coming of Jesus Christ (Art. 18); in the bodily resurrection of the dead (Art. 19); in final judgment (Art. 20); and in heaven and hell (Art. 21).

As the center, orthodoxy is the key interpretive lens through which Wesleyans have read difficult biblical texts and formed Christian doctrine. Therefore, when confronted with the Arian debate about Jesus Christ—whether Christ is God or an exalted creature—Wesleyans have followed the orthodox reading of Scripture, confessing Jesus as fully divine, the eternal Son of the Father, and have interpreted unclear passages in the New Testament which appear to challenge Christ's deity from that perspective.

Any theological reading of Scripture that violates orthodoxy's doctrines has been rejected by Wesleyans and viewed as a rejection of essential Christian beliefs. Orthodoxy forms an interpretive boundary that must not be crossed theologically. As such, orthodoxy forms the "rule of faith" in doctrinal interpretation of the Bible.

Extending immediately from the center circle is the Protestant tradition of the church. The Protestant perspective fleshes out in greater detail the rudiments of Christian doctrine established by orthodoxy and at some points distinguishes the Wesleyan theological hermeneutic from approaches taken by Roman Catholicism and/or Eastern Orthodoxy. As aligned with Protestantism, the Wesleyan doctrine and "analogy of faith" is shaped by the following emphases in The Wesleyan Church's Articles: humanity's total depravity apart from grace (Art. 8), the divine initiative in salvation (Art. 8), personal conversion/new birth (Art. 11), salvation by grace through faith (Art. 11), good works as the fruit of regeneration (Art. 12), the evangelical marks of the church (Art. 16), and the two sacraments of baptism and Holy Communion (Art. 17).

While some Wesleyan/Holiness sects, denominations, and leaders have rejected key aspects of Protestantism's "analogy of faith"—e.g., the practice of spiritual sacraments by the Salvation Army, and Charles Finney's Pelagian views of original sin—they do not define the mainstream of Wesleyan doctrinal thought. As a whole, the Protestant distinctives derived from its theological reading of the Bible play a guiding role in the formation of Wesleyan doctrine. For example, when addressing the issue of whether a person has the natural ability to exercise faith in salvation or must have divine grace to enable saving faith, Wesleyans have followed the Protestant reading of relevant biblical texts and argued for the absolute necessity of God's grace.

Finally, the last ring forming the Wesleyan view of the "whole of Scripture" has its sources in the British Wesleyan and the American Holiness Movements of the eighteenth, nineteenth, and twentieth centuries. This theological reading clarifies further the Wesleyan doctrine set forth in its orthodox and Protestant understanding. Most notably, it gives voice to an irrepressible optimism in the power of God's grace to save and "save to the uttermost," while also emphasizing appropriate human cooperation with grace. More specifically, the Wesleyan distinctives, exemplified in The Wesleyan Church's Articles, include: love as the chief end of humanity (Art. 6), prevenient grace (Art. 8), unlimited atonement (Art. 9), a high view of regeneration/new birth (Art. 11), the possibility of "falling from grace" (Art. 13), and entire sanctification (Art. 14).

Therefore, as Wesleyans have engaged in biblical study and articulated their particular perspectives on a number of debated theological issues in Christianity, they have identified a different set of "clear passages" than other Protestants through which to interpret the Bible in the construction of doctrine. This tradition forms the defining interpretive lens for the Wesleyan "analogy of faith." For example, Wesleyans believe the perfect love of God and neighbor is the chief end of humanity. As such, humanity is created primarily for relationship with God and with other human beings. While this teaching does not directly oppose the dominant Reformed understanding, stated in the Westminster Catechism as "to glorify God," the difference has implications in and for the Wesleyan account of salvation and sanctification. Thus, when confronted on the question of a Christian's victory over sin in the present life (our second example at the beginning of this chapter), Wesleyans assert that Scripture teaches God's grace can free people from the bondage of sin and empower them to love God and neighbor.

THE CONTINUING WORK OF INTERPRETING THE BIBLE'S THEOLOGY

Perhaps, at this point, one of the most essential aspects of the doctrinal reading of Scripture should be discussed in greater detail. Christian theology is shaped by doctrinal development in its articulation of the Christian faith and is committed to contributing further growth when appropriate.

First, Christian doctrine acknowledges the Bible as the written Word of God, but recognizes it has taken the church centuries to probe its depths, to apprehend more fully the divine revelation given, and to flesh out its implications. The theological enterprise seeks not only to state what Scripture has ratified and defined, but also to what it points. Christian creeds, confessions of faith, and articles of religion often state logical developments of seminal ideas in the biblical testimony. The doctrine of the Trinity and the deity of the Holy Spirit have been given already as models of this type of doctrinal development.

Another example is the orthodox understanding of the humanity of Christ. The Scriptures clearly teach that Christ became incarnate. But did this mean Christ simply took a physical body, or did it entail a human soul as well? The New Testament does not have a polished discussion of the subject. However, as the New Testament's testimony on Christ's humanity was studied, and the implications of the incarnation became a subject of deep reflection, over time, the church developed a doctrine of the full humanity of Christ—body and soul. This then became a part of the developing "analogy of faith" by which the Scriptures were read in the orthodox tradition.

Second, Christian theology is dedicated to continued reflection and development of Christian doctrine in the church. Therefore, theologians continue to reflect upon the key doctrines of the church, such as the Trinity, the full humanity of Christ, and the atonement, as well as doctrinal distinctives, such as entire sanctification.

But this is not an unrestrained or completely speculative venture. Rather, it's one with established parameters, following the clear trajectories established by orthodoxy in its readings of the biblical text. Just as there is growth in the development of the human body from infancy to adulthood, just as there is growth of a plant from seed to maturity, so, too, the church develops in her understanding of God's truth given in Scripture. As a rule, this entails gaining further insight into what was previously expressed in general terms or only acknowledged as true, or in clarifying what was understood only obscurely. The essential nature of a given doctrine remains intact, while its understanding and implications are developed more fully.

For example, contemporary Wesleyan reflection on the doctrine of the Trinity is focusing on what it is to be a person. The whole vocabulary of "person" and "personhood" is not found in the Bible, but in the Trinitarian doctrinal developments of the fourth and fifth centuries of the church. Wesleyan theologians, in dialogue with the biblical text and with Christian orthodoxy, are exploring how understanding the Father, Son, and Holy Spirit as divine persons can help us see more clearly what it is for us to be constituted as human persons.

One insight gained from this study is that a human person, theologically understood, is not an isolated self, but is communal in nature. To be truly a person, a human being must be rightly related in love to God and other human beings. Of course, nothing here contradicts either Scripture or orthodoxy, but it does help us understand the biblical witness more deeply.

SUMMARY AND CONCLUSION

In summary, because the Scriptures contain an overarching narrative of God and God's relationship with the created order, there exists within them coherent theological themes about God, creation, fall, redemption, and consummation. The task of Christian theology is to give a faithful, cohesive account of these doctrinal themes.

But this enterprise is not as simple as it may appear initially. There are challenges to be faced and we see their fruit in the common doctrinal debates over biblical teaching. Christian theology begins in humble recognition of these challenges and its absolute dependency on the Holy Spirit's illumination working through the church.

To read the Scriptures doctrinally, theology looks at the whole of biblical teaching on the major theological themes of Scripture, and not just at some part(s) of it. Then, the "whole of Scripture" becomes the lens through which difficult or unclear passages are read. Specifically, The Wesleyan Church account of the Bible's theology has been shaped by its prayerful dialogue and reflection upon Scripture with three faith communities—orthodox, Protestant, and Wesleyan/Holiness—and is expressed in her Articles of Religion.

Finally, the work of Christian theology is not static. Clear, disciplined doctrinal development is evident throughout the history of the church, and work continues within the body of Christ to clarify and develop the theology given to us in the Holy Scriptures.

ACTION/REFLECTION SUGGESTIONS

1. Identify a specific moment in your life when you came across doctrinal or theological teaching, "based on Scripture," with which you disagreed. Why did you disagree with it?

2. Think of a difficult passage of Scripture you've had trouble reconciling with other passages. Based on this chapter, what might be some of the issues involved and how would you approach this passage theologically?

3. Find copies of the Apostles' and Nicene Creeds. As you read them, identify the outline of the biblical story—God, creation, fall, redemption, and consummation. What do the creeds say specifically about each of these biblical themes?

4. Because the Apostles' and Nicene Creeds form an interpretive boundary or "rule of faith" that must not be crossed in theological interpretation, commit both creeds to memory, if you haven't already.

FOR FURTHER READING

Drury, Keith. *Common Ground: What All Christians Believe and Why It Matters.* Indianapolis: Wesleyan Publishing House, 2008.

This is an easy-to-understand introduction to the Apostles' Creed, exploring its meaning and significance for Christians today. If you have little or no knowledge about the significance of a "rule of faith" in biblical interpretation, Keith Drury's book is the place to start.

Dunning, H. Ray. *Grace, Faith and Holiness: A Wesleyan Systematic Theology.* Kansas City, Mo.: Beacon Hill, 1988.

This is a more difficult book for those without a background in theology. However, it does provide an extensive discussion of theological method in the Wesleyan tradition, as well as a developed treatment of Christian doctrine.

Greathouse, William, and H. Ray Dunning. *An Introduction to Wesleyan Theology.* Kansas City, Mo.: Beacon Hill, 1988.

Greathouse and Dunning provide a concise overview of Christian doctrine from a Wesleyan perspective. They examine Christian essentials while addressing Wesleyan distinctives. This is an excellent follow-up to Drury's book for those in the Wesleyan-Arminian tradition.

McGrath, Alister E. *Studies in Doctrine: Understanding Doctrine, Understanding the Trinity, Understanding Jesus, Justification by Faith.* Grand Rapids: Zondervan, 1997.

Here McGrath gives an excellent overview of doctrinal development—how we move from the Bible to the central doctrines of the Christian faith. It's understandable, written for an educated laity.

McGrath, Alister E. *The Genesis of Doctrine: A Study in the Foundation of Doctrinal Criticism.* Vancouver, B.C: Regent College Publishing, 1997.

This is a more advanced treatment of doctrinal development for people with theological training. However, if you are seeking a detailed study of doctrinal hermeneutics, McGrath's book is the best.

9

INSPIRATION

Gareth Lee Cockerill

*But the word is very near you. It is in your mouth and in
your heart, so that you can do it.*

—Deuteronomy 30:14 (ESV)

God speaks not as man, but as God. His thoughts are very deep: and hence
his words are of inexhaustible virtue. And the language of his messengers
also is exact in the highest degree: for the words which were given them
accurately answered the impression made upon their minds.

—John Wesley

G od has spoken to human beings enmeshed in the circumstances
of earthly life (Heb. 1:1–2; 2 Tim. 3:16). The fact that Scripture
is both divine and human is of supreme importance. Only such a
Scripture is in accord with the rest of the Christian faith; only through
such a Scripture can God accomplish his purposes for humanity; and
only such a Scripture suffices for the deep need of women and men.

ONLY A DIVINE-HUMAN SCRIPTURE COULD REFLECT THE MYSTERY OF THE CHRISTIAN FAITH

The divinity and humanity of Scripture must always be understood in light of the incarnation of the Son of God to whom Scripture bears witness. "The Word became flesh and dwelt among us" (John 1:14 ESV). "Since then the children share in flesh and blood, he himself took on the same" (Heb. 2:14, author's translation). "Therefore he had to be made like his sisters and brothers in every respect" (Heb. 2:17, author's translation). At the heart of the Christian faith is the fact that the Son of God became fully human without ceasing to be the Son of God. The Christian church carefully worked out the expression of this biblical truth during the first centuries of its existence. Jesus Christ is not part God and part human, but fully God and fully human—yet he is one person. This impenetrable mystery is indeed the treasure of the Christian faith.

All God's dealings with humanity anticipate or reflect the incarnation of his Son. From the beginning God revealed himself by becoming intimately involved in human life. He met with Adam and Eve in the garden (Gen. 3:8). He called Abraham and gave him a promise (Gen. 12:1–3; 15:1–6). He delivered his people from slavery (Ex. 4:18—14:31) and spoke to them at Sinai (Ex. 20:1–26). He took the ancient, human covenant form and used it as a basis for his relationship with those he had redeemed (Gen. 15:7–21; Ex. 20:1–26). He employed every form of human speech—story, song, and parable—to communicate with them. In fulfillment of his promise to Abraham he entered into an ongoing relationship with the human race that found its climax in Jesus Christ (cf. Gal. 3:14).

The Bible is the book that records this grand history of God's self-revelation culminating in Jesus Christ. Thus, in line with the way God has always revealed himself and in accord with the Christ to whom it bears witness, the Bible is both divine and human. The Son of God took on our humanity without ceasing to be the Son of God. In Scripture the "word" of God took on human speech without ceasing to be the "word" of God. As the divine-human Son remained one person, so the divine-human word remains one act of communication.

ONLY A DIVINE-HUMAN SCRIPTURE COULD ACCOMPLISH THE PURPOSES OF A LOVING GOD

The importance of this truth comes into focus when we grasp God's purpose in revealing himself. God created humanity in God's own image, that human beings might have intimate, interpersonal fellowship with him. Genesis 3:1–20 describes the repudiation of God through which humans were alienated from their divine benefactor. The rest of Scripture relates the story of God's restoring that fellowship. Every interpersonal relationship requires involvement in the life of the other person. So God has become intimately involved in human life in order to renew our fellowship with him. In the second century, St. Irenaeus expressed the intimacy of God's involvement when he said that only what Christ assumed could be redeemed. Christ had to take on full humanity in order that humanity might be brought back into fellowship with God.

The result of this process is the book in which God's own self-revelation has become fully enmeshed in human life, thought, and language, so all people may be restored to fellowship with God. It will be helpful to compare this book with the Qu'ran. According to the Bible, God reveals his character so people might come into fellowship with him. According to the Qu'ran, God reveals the laws he has arbitrarily established so people might conform to them. Thus the Qu'ran is not the result of God's intimate involvement in all the variety of human life, but of God's dictating his laws through the prophet. The Qu'ranic model is dictation, not incarnation. We might describe the Muslim view of the Qu'ran as fully divine but minimally human. Much more is required to bring humans into fellowship with the living God.

ONLY A DIVINE-HUMAN SCRIPTURE COULD MEET THE NEEDS OF THE PEOPLE OF GOD

If a divine-human Scripture was necessary for God to redeem humanity, it was essential for the needs of God's people. In this section, however, we celebrate the rich variety of ways God has involved himself with human culture throughout Scripture. By employing this diversity he has made his truth accessible, and thus fellowship with him available, in all cultures, time periods, and stages of life.

The Bible was not written just for my culture and me. Some things that seem odd to us are perfectly understandable to someone on another continent or from a different century. Abraham's bargaining with the Hittites for a burial place (Gen. 23) seems strange to Westerners, but is perfectly comprehensible to many in the East. Many secular-minded Christians in the West are embarrassed by Jesus' casting out evil spirits. However, many from other parts of the world recognize the reality of such things and find Jesus' power over them fundamental to salvation. Affluent moderns may need to hear, "Honor your father and your mother." People in developing countries where family loyalty is strong but corruption is rife may need, "You shall not bear false witness." A young person may find the emphasis of Psalm 90 on the brevity of life depressing. One approaching life's end is reassured by the same psalm's emphasis on God's faithfulness.

Some detract from our Bible because of this great variety. They scoff, saying it's full of contradictions. They fail to see beyond its humanity to its deity. So people scoffed at our Lord and refused to believe he was anything more than human. We, however, celebrate the human variety of Scripture because it is God's means of making his message relevant to every aspect of human life.

INTERPRETING A BIBLE BOTH HUMAN AND DIVINE

If the Bible truly is both human and divine, God's word assuming human speech without ceasing to be God's word, then it must be interpreted accordingly. We must be sensitive to the normal human character of Scripture's language without losing sight of its divine message. We must take into consideration human limitation without surrendering divine truth. We must not violate what God has bound together by trying to extract the divine from the human.

A DIVINE MESSAGE EXPRESSED IN HUMAN SPEECH

The person who would understand Scripture must give attention to the normal conventions of human speech without losing sight of the divine message. Many violations of this principle are common in the church. We laugh at those who posit secret "codes" in the Bible, yet fall into the trap of thinking the language of Scripture has more meaning than normal language or communicates meaning in unusual ways. We are saved from this error if we seek to understand Scripture's teaching as its original hearers understood it.

Overreliance on a word's family tree is a common violation of this principle. Usually, we are unaware of where the words we hear came from. The way we hear them used, not their derivation, determines our understanding of their meaning. But when it comes to the Bible, some lose sight of this principle, even going so far as to define New Testament words by their twentieth-century descendents. Who has not heard someone say that "dynamite" comes from *dunamis*, the Greek word for "power"? Therefore, when the New Testament speaks of the *dunamis* of God, it's speaking of the "dynamite" of God. But the first New Testament readers had no knowledge of dynamite; the etymological derivation of the modern English word is not a legitimate explanation of the ancient Greek word. Moreover, when we hear others speak in our day-to-day lives, we never use such principles to understand their words.

Another fallacy occurs when we argue that the same word used in two different contexts must have the same meaning. Perhaps you have heard someone say something like this: "The Greek term for *word* in Hebrews 4:12–13 is *logos*, the same word used in John 1:1. Since *logos* refers to the Son of God in John 1:1, it also must refer to him in Hebrews 4:12–13." Now, the Greek word *logos* is as general as the English word for *word*. Its use in both places is no more significant than the fact that English translations use "word" in both verses. The context of John 1:1–14 gives *logos*/"word" a specialized meaning not clearly present elsewhere in the New Testament.

DIVINE ACCURACY RECORDED WITHIN HUMAN LIMITATION

"God is a God of truth. God has spoken in Scripture. Therefore the Bible must be completely true." How often have you heard someone make such a statement? It's logically compelling. Logic, however, is only as good as the adequacy of the facts upon which it is based. The above statement needs qualification because it does not include all the facts. It encompasses the divinity but not the humanity of Scripture. Let us remedy this situation: "God is a God of truth. God has spoken by entering human life and revealing himself in the human language of Scripture. Therefore the Bible must be completely true within the human constraints of its context." Granted, such a statement is subject to misuse (as are most statements). Yet, to ignore the humanity of Scripture leads to aberrant interpretation.

Let's look at a couple of examples. Some have suffered deep distress because Jesus said the mustard seed was the smallest seed (Matt.

13:31–32), although modern science has discovered smaller. A moment's reflection will show that had Jesus exercised infinite knowledge about such subjects as biology during his earthly life, his humanity would have been something very different from ours. His very mission necessitated accepting this limitation. The mustard seed was the smallest seed with which his hearers were familiar. If he had named some unknown small seed his message would have been incomprehensible to them. Within the human context of that moment, Jesus communicated the truth of God with perfect accuracy.

A second example is more difficult. Some have struggled with the minor apparent contradictions between the Gospels. Matthew 26:34, 74–75; Luke 22:34, 60– 61; and John 13:38; 18:27 record that Peter denied Jesus three times before the cock crowed. Mark 14:30, 68, and 72, however, say he denied Jesus three times before the cock crowed twice. Matthew reported that Jesus cast demons from two demoniacs beyond the Sea of Galilee (8:28–34), and healed two blind men as he approached Jerusalem (20:29–34). Mark and Luke, however, record his casting demons from only one man (Mark 5:1–17; Luke 8:26–37) and healing only one (Mark 10:46–52; Luke 18:35–43).

How can we account for such differences? It's important to remember that God intended the Gospels to represent eyewitness testimony to Jesus (John 20:30).[1] The very mark of truthful witnesses is general agreement with variation in details. Total unanimity betrays collaboration. Thus God intended these documents to present a truthful picture of Jesus without compromising their evidentiary value as eyewitness testimony.

DIVINE WORD UNITED WITH HUMAN WORD

God is the one who has joined his word to the human word of Scripture to make his truth applicable to the human race. We must not separate the two. We may be tempted to extract the divine message from the human word because of things in Scripture that seem strange or repulsive. It's easy to say, "Well, that was only cultural and therefore it is no longer applicable." We must resist this temptation. It's true that some things must be applied differently in different cultures. We must not, however, discard the human embodiment of the divine word. Where our circumstances differ, that embodiment is a model and guide for application in our situation. The vast variety of the cultural contexts in which God has revealed himself in Scripture is a resource for the continual relevance of his truth. The divine message we extract when we discard the human husk almost certainly will not be the message God intended.

OLD TESTAMENT EXAMPLES

Of course, many seeming difficulties in Scripture, especially those in the Old Testament, are clarified by understanding their significance within the larger canon of Scripture.[2] Let me give a couple of examples, however, of how the human context of Scripture helps us apply Scripture's truth in our own altered environment.

The Ten Commandments (Ex. 20:1–17) rightly are given prominence in Christian nurture. They were spoken by God from the mountain and are an expression of his character. They are the fundamental principles upon which God established his covenant at Sinai.

But what about all the other laws in the Pentateuch that told Israel how to live in the Promised Land under primitive conditions as a society structured around family and clan? It does little good to try to apply many of these laws one by one. They are part of a larger system. God was using this whole system to shape Israel into a society that would reflect his character in the world. Thus we can study them as a whole within their ancient context, to see what kind of society God was shaping, so we can shape our own lives accordingly.

For instance, the laws dealing with money and land were intended to ensure that all would share in the economic resources necessary for life. These laws checked greed without condoning indolence. A person who through misfortune sunk into poverty would borrow money from those better off. The law instructed those with means to lend without charging interest, for interest only would have put a greater burden on the poor (Ex. 22:25; Lev. 25:36–37; Deut. 23:19). Creditors could not keep the debtor's cloak overnight in pledge for money, lest he suffer from cold (Ex. 22:26–27; Deut. 24:13).

If the unfortunate person continued to sink further into debt, he and his land could be sold in order to pay. Even then, however, the one who bought him was to treat him well. Moreover, every fiftieth year was the Year of Jubilee, in which all slaves were freed and all agricultural land was returned to its original owner (Lev. 25:8–17, 23–55; 27:16–25; Num. 36:4). The one who had bought the debtor was to be generous with him, furnishing the newly freed slave with the necessities to restart his life. Thus, all were assured of continual participation in needed resources. These provisions kept great wealth from accumulating permanently in the hands of a few. Our question becomes: How can we structure our own social life according to these principles?[3]

NEW TESTAMENT EXAMPLES

The previous lengthy example is from the Old Testament. A simple New Testament example is the instruction for Christians to give each other "a holy kiss" (Rom. 16:16; 1 Cor. 16:20; 2 Cor. 13:12; 1 Thess. 5:26; 1 Pet. 5:14). In some societies today people kiss when greeting one another—usually men to men and women to women. In others, the kiss is reserved only for sexual relations. It's necessary to determine what function the "holy kiss" fulfilled in the New Testament church and to find an equivalent expression of that function for churches in other cultures. That kiss probably expressed the mutual relationship between Christians as brothers and sisters in Christ who harbored no unforgiveness toward one another. Every society will have an appropriate way to express this relationship.

I have saved the most difficult example for last. There can be no doubt that the gospel has transformed the relationship between women and men. First of all, it's clear that all share equally in salvation (Gal. 3:28). All participate in the gift of the Holy Spirit (Acts 2:17). Such transformation was bound to have beneficial social consequences. Thus we have Paul affirming that women have sexual rights over their husbands' bodies just as much as men have over their wives' (1 Cor. 7:1–5). This may seem obvious to us, but Paul was speaking in an environment where men of privilege routinely had concubines for nightly copulation, paramours for lovers, and wives for legitimate children.

Nor was there anything in the ancient world like Paul's admonition for husbands to love their wives as Christ loves the church (Eph. 5:25–33). Husbands were not to love their wives because they were beautiful, but to make them beautiful by their love. They were to be devoted to their wives' welfare and even willing to die for their benefit.

And yet it's clear from many New Testament passages that the Bible enjoined distinctions in the roles played by men and women, particularly by husbands and wives. The husband is to be devoted to the wife and the wife is to submit to the husband (Eph. 5:22–24, 33; 1 Pet. 3:1–6). Other, somewhat enigmatic, passages seem to put restrictions on women's teaching in the church (1 Cor. 14:34–35; 1 Tim. 2:11–15).

We no longer live in a society built on the extended family. New Testament people lived in a world where the household was the major economic unit—the place where clothes and food were produced, the young were instructed, and the aged were cared for. We live in a time when women have equal access to education and to the professions. And yet we live in a time when abuse and mistreatment abound. Thus we must struggle in our own world to find ways in which the transforming power of the gospel determines this most fundamental of human relationships. At the same time, we must find appropriate ways to affirm the difference and mutual dependence between men and women also enjoined by the New Testament.

CONCLUSION

The humanity and divinity of Scripture is indeed a treasure. Because the Bible is both divine and human, it truly reveals God to us in such a way that we can enter into fellowship with him. His truth can impact all of life, in every society and condition. How important when we open such a treasure that we use the jewels found therein in accord with the giver's intention!

ACTION/REFLECTION SUGGESTIONS

1. When you read Scripture, pay attention to its human character. Note its literary forms, its beauty, its use of metaphors, and its poetry.

2. Along with the above suggestion, always ask what a passage is teaching about God and our relationship with him.

3. With each reading, praise God with awe and thanksgiving because he has made himself available to us human beings.

FOR FURTHER READING

Bauckham, Richard. *Bible and Mission: Christian Witness in a Postmodern World*. Grand Rapids: Baker Academic, 2003.

Bauckham contends the Bible is God's word for the whole world. He shows how the gospel message is definitive for all human cultures in the postmodern pluralistic contemporary world.

Bauckham, Richard. *Jesus and the Eyewitnesses: The Gospels as Eyewitness Testimony.* Grand Rapids: Eerdmans, 2006.

Are the four gospels based on the testimony of those who were eyewitness to the life of Jesus? This book presents a refreshing, creative, and clear argument for an affirmative answer. The Gospels are both human eyewitness testimony and the word of God.

Wright, Christopher J. H. *Old Testament Ethics for the People of God.* Downers Grove, Ill.: InterVarsity Press, 2004.

The Old Testament law was God's word given to human beings who lived in the ancient world before the coming of Christ. The author seeks to show how it continues to be God's word for contemporary human life.

NOTES

1. See Richard Bauckham, *Jesus and the Eyewitnesses: The Gospels as Eyewitness Testimony* (Grand Rapids: Eerdmans, 2006).

2. See Gareth Lee Cockerill, "Heaven Opened: Unity of Scripture," in Joseph Coleson, ed., *Passion, Power, and Purpose: Essays on the Art of Contemporary Preaching* (Indianapolis: Wesleyan Publishing House, 2006), 111–24; cf. also several chapters within this present book.

3. For this way of approaching the Old Testament law, see Christopher J. H. Wright, *Old Testament Ethics for the People of God* (Downers Grove, Ill.: InterVarsity Press, 2004).

10

PROGRESSIVE REVELATION

D. Darek Jarmola

Where there is no revelation, the people perish.

— Proverbs 29:18 (author's translation)

If thine heart is as my heart, if thou lovest God and all
mankind, I ask no more: give me thine hand.

—John Wesley

O n the surface, there seems to be a contradiction between the
Christian understanding of God's nature and attributes as eternal
and unchanging, and his "progressive revelation" recorded in the
Scriptures. Some struggle with the concept of God who is "the same
yesterday, today, and tomorrow," yet whose story is recorded in the
Bible in terms that appear to be unfolding, changing, and emergent.
How can one profess an unchanging God who uses a progressive story
to reveal himself?

Within the Bible one may notice a motif of development of God's
teaching about humanity's relationship with the Creator, and our

relationships with each other. Records of doctrinal, moral, and ethical teachings had to begin at an elementary level, because ancient Israel was the beginning of God's working out of his redemptive purposes in this world. This chapter suggests that an understanding of God's nature and his teachings requires us to read the Bible in the context of the whole of God's recorded revelation, not just in the situational revelations found in any one book, section, or pericope.

GOD IN A CHANGING WORLD

Genesis 1:1–2 presents God as the uncreated Creator who intentionally and purposefully produced a temporal and finite world, beginning a changing and evolving relationship with his own creation. Here, the paradoxical concepts of constant and change met for the first time.

In the creation story, humanity first met God, who is Trinity. Yet, it was only over time that God the Trinity fully revealed himself to his creation. For most of the Old Testament story, humans experienced God the Father and, to a lesser degree, God the Holy Spirit. God revealed himself more completely in the person of Jesus of Nazareth; in the pages of the New Testament, God's redemptive purpose is finally and fully revealed. Here, also, the final dimension of God's nature is revealed, with purposeful and more complete teaching on the person and work of the Holy Spirit.

However, the idea of the eternal Creator entering into and becoming a part of the story of humankind raises a question: how can a changing human history—always confined to time and space—capture, record, and present the Creator, who is not bound by time and space? This question becomes more significant when put alongside the fact that the record of God's self-revelation in human history was produced by imperfect, time-and-space-bound human beings.

Even more startling is the fact that the view of history recorded by the Scriptures is in direct contrast to the views of two dominant neighboring civilizations also present in the pages of the Old Testament, namely, Mesopotamia and Egypt.[1] Against their pessimistic and stagnant views of reality and history, the biblical story presents a radically different understanding. The Bible reports a God who chooses to redefine history in terms that are progressive—there is a beginning and an end to human history; intentional—there is a purpose to our history; and positive—the best part of the story is yet to be written. Accordingly, the God revealed on the pages of the Bible is an active, positive, and necessary participant in the progressive story of humanity. However, even as God is fully present in all of human history, the record of that progressive presence is mostly limited to the stories recorded in the pages of the Old and New Testaments. Ironically, modern understanding of historical records and their validity is often at odds with the biblical view of history.

One must recognize that God's concept of time is different from that of human beings. To record history, humans must have an understanding of time and space. The ancient Greeks referred to this concept as *chronos*, meaning time before and after. From this Greek word we derive a number of time-related English terms, e.g., "chronicle" and "chronology." The most important characteristic of *chronos* is that it can be captured and measured. This concept of time can be "accounted for." Events within it are experienced, and can be known and recorded. "History" is a record of human events over time.

However, one of God's attributes is timelessness. God does not have a beginning; there was no time when God was not. In more doctrinal terms, God is before time was! Thus, it's very important to note that the Bible records God's entry into human history by using the Greek word *kairos* (Mark 1:15), not *chronos*. *Kairos* is a special, unique, present moment in human history. The most important characteristic of *kairos* is that it cannot be measured; *kairos* refers to the ever-present "now" moment in time. Yet, when Paul spoke of Christ's entry into temporal, finite human history, he said, "The time (*chronos*) had fully come" (Gal. 4:4). Here *chronos* and *kairos* meet; here the eternal God reveals himself more fully in temporal, time-bound, human history. Here, also, one faces the question of how the Bible is God's history in the midst of the human story.

One of the most constructive concepts for explaining God's story within the human story in the pages of the Bible is the German term *Heilsgeschichte*. This term most often is translated "salvation history" or "redemptive history," but a more literal translation is "holy history." *Heilsgeschichte* refers to God's stories recorded in the Bible, and also makes clear these stories are told from the divine viewpoint. As such, they are different from a merely human understanding of history, past or present. The Bible is a perfect record of God's holy history, recorded within progressive human history.[2]

With this approach, we can accept the existence of the unchanging, eternal God who yet interacts in an ever-changing, process-driven, human history. This approach also can credit the fact of missing historical details in biblical stories, without their lack destroying the overall validity or importance of the existing biblical record. For example, one can accept that the known records about the historical Jesus are incomplete—the Bible has records only of Jesus' birth, his visit to the temple at age twelve, and his years of ministry; records of his childhood and young adulthood are missing—without doubting Jesus' historicity or the redemptive nature of his ministry.

GOD CHANGING THE WORLD

God's progressive work in human history is illustrated by the concept of the covenant. The first hint of this covenant is found in Genesis 12, when God made a verbal promise to Abraham. God promised to consecrate and to accept this particular individual, and later his descendents, as God's agents in bringing all humanity into the divine realm.

With Moses, the covenant relationship moved from a verbal to a written stage. From Mount Sinai onward, the Ten Commandments and the rest of the Torah constituted the numerous lessons necessary to understand better God's contract with God's people. Following the often disheartening events of the wilderness wanderings, Israel (under Joshua) began to experience the fulfillment of the verbal promises made to Abraham centuries before. Later, and notwithstanding their shortcomings, David and Solomon experienced the extension of God's covenant to their dynastic line, and began the proclamation from Jerusalem of the broader covenant embodied in the Torah, even to some nations and people groups beyond Israel. (See 1 Kings 4:29–34; 10:1–13.)

The Old Testament story often became a record of disappointments following the death of Solomon. Centuries later, as a remnant of Judeans was being carried into exile in other lands, Jeremiah spoke of a new covenant that would "put [God's] law in their minds and write it on their *hearts*" (Jer. 31:33, emphasis added). The context of this spiritual covenant Jeremiah also recorded: "They will be my people, and I will be their God. I will give them singleness of heart and action, so that they will always fear me for their own good and the good of their children after them. I will make an everlasting covenant with them" (Jer. 32:38–40).

This progression from a verbal, to a written, to a spiritual bond was picked up by Paul and early Christian apologists, who showed that because God's relationship is written on the heart, it's directly available to all people. Yet, it is important to note that even when dealing with Abraham and Moses, God had spoken of his covenant as a "work in progress" involving all people, and not just Israelites.

In other words, there is only one comprehensive covenant, but its meaning and nature are revealed progressively.

One can recognize that the covenant between God and all humanity has been of paramount importance all along, but it's made explicit in those terms only at the end of the biblical story. One can see that the covenant does not mean any particular Jew is more beloved of God than any particular Gentile. God desires a relationship with all because each person has value.

Moreover, the political reality of the Davidic kingdom was not replaced by the spiritual reality of the New Testament *ekklesia*. Rather, there is only one biblical concept of the kingdom of God, first revealed via the theocratic monarchy of Israel, then predicted in a new form by the prophets, preached by Jesus, and finally taught by the apostles. That concept of God's kingdom is present throughout the biblical story, but is fully revealed only with the appearance of Jesus.

JESUS CHRIST AS THE AGENT OF GOD'S REVELATION

The kingdom of God concept points to the progressive nature of God's relationship with his creation. Starting with Abraham, God's redemptive history progressed from the story of the Hebrews into the stories involving the Gentiles. From the very beginning, the record of the Bible shows God's intention to offer redemption to all humanity. Yet, the story starts with a single individual from Mesopotamia and moves on to the single nation group from Canaan, before it can be understood as the redemptive story for all humanity.

Here is where we recognize Jesus as the most direct, real, and substantive revelation of the God who created the universe. In Jesus, progressive revelation is both affirmed and explained; in the person of Christ, God's purpose and character are fully revealed to the world. Looking to Jesus, human beings may know not only that God's revelation is progressive, but also that it is future-bound because of God's love for us. As such, God's progressive revelation leads humanity to a better understanding of salvation.

At the same time, God's revelation through the story of Jesus is for the whole of reality. In practical terms, this means that even as the biblical story reveals that God's truth and love are universal, so, also, is human freedom. The reality of human freedom is validated by and in Christ. Given this perspective, we can find God's revelation even in natural, personal, and historical events outside the Bible; a category that theologians sometimes label "natural revelation." (See Ps. 19:1–6; Rom. 1:19–20; 10:20—Paul's citation of Isa. 65:1.)

Yet, such an approach also brings us to the problem of religious pluralism, the claim that God is equally present in all religions. The one corrective response here is that the focal point of God's progressive revelation is Jesus, especially the event of his resurrection. While the starting point for the nature of Christ is the historical Jesus of Nazareth, his life and his death, Jesus' resurrection is the dominant, ultimate, and defining event of God's revelation to us. One may go so far as to combine both events as necessary, for without the historical resurrection of Jesus, no logical explanation of the ministry of Jesus' disciples, and of the emergence of the church, is possible.

However, the claims of the historical resurrection demand more than we can see without the eyes of faith. This is because the resurrection is the act of God, not of Jesus or anybody else; only God the Creator could do it. The resurrection of Jesus is a *novum* event in God's progressive history, a divine act reaching into human reality and history. It's the event that clarifies and explains God's progressive revelation as both soteriological and eschatological in its nature, scope, and goals.

LEX TALIONIS: AN EXAMPLE OF PROGRESSIVE REVELATION

The Sermon on the Mount validates God's past revelations, "the Law [and] the Prophets," and claims, as its sole aim, helping people understand their original purpose (Matt. 5:17). According to Matthew 22:37–40, the aim of the Law was to set people free by teaching love of God (vertical relationship) and love of neighbor (horizontal relationship). Here, in Jesus' explanation of the Law's original purpose, we find some of the best illustrations of the nature of God's progressive revelation. Jesus called attention to four aspects of the Law— murder, adultery, oaths, and retaliation—to show the progressive steps needed to arrive at their full meaning and comprehensive intention. For brevity's sake, we will examine here only the law of retaliation.

"You have heard that it was said, 'Eye for eye, and tooth for tooth.' But I tell you, Do not resist an evil person. If someone strikes you on the right cheek, turn to him the other also" (Matt. 5:38–39). Here, in Jesus' teaching, is the final revelation of God's own heart, which calls upon humanity to love universally and selflessly in both horizontal and vertical relationships.

To appreciate fully this example of God's progressive revelation, we must take a few steps back, noting how each previous phase progressed toward God's final purpose as revealed by Jesus' sermon. Clarence Jordan has summed it up: first was the way of unlimited retaliation; then the process moved to limited retaliation; next, the way of limited love was introduced; and, finally, the fullness of God's intent is seen in Jesus' teaching about unlimited love.[3]

The oldest way of dealing with enemies is the way of unlimited retaliation. By this principle, if someone hurts you, you are free to hurt him back, with scarcely any limitations. For example, Hammurabi's Code (from Babylon, about 1750 B.C.) required that damages be repaid tenfold, or even more; moreover, for many offenses the sentence was death. In effect, few limits were placed on retribution. Such a principle, unmitigated, can tend only to the escalation of violence and cycles of constant retribution; it would lead eventually to the destruction of humanity.

This principle was superseded by the Law given to Moses. Exodus 21:23–25 (see also Lev. 24:20; Deut. 19:21) states, "You are to take life for life, eye for eye, tooth for tooth, hand for hand, foot for foot, burn for burn, wound for wound, bruise for bruise." God's law calls for limited retribution; vengeance may equal the original crime, but may not exceed it. Obviously, this was a major improvement over unlimited retribution. It's important to note, too, that most modern definitions of justice are based on this limited retribution principle.

However, even this principle was replaced already in the Torah. In Leviticus 19:18, God said, "Do not seek revenge or bear a grudge against one of your people, but love your neighbor as yourself." Jesus quoted this text in his Sermon on the Mount. His reference to "hate your enemy" (Matt. 5:43), reflects the common first-century perception of "your neighbor" as "another Jew." According to this principle of "limited love," forgiveness is better than retaliation, as long as the offender belongs to the same nationality, ethnicity, and/or religious group. Thus, a Jew might forgive another Jew for an injustice, but retaliate against a non-Jew who committed a similar offense. Greeks, Romans, and others often did the same.

This principle suggests boundaries to goodwill and forgiveness are necessary, and the best place to draw them is at one's religious, ethnic, or national identity. An obvious (unintended?) consequence is that it creates a double standard for forgiveness and retaliation. The same transgression may result in understanding and forgiveness for one from the "in crowd," but in retribution inflicted upon outsiders. Historically, this is what happened to Jews in Hitler's Germany, and to African slaves in the United States.

The Sermon on the Mount brings the concept of retribution to its intended conclusion. Jesus said, "But I am telling you: Love the outsider and pray for those who attack you, so that you might be sons of your heavenly Father" (Matt. 5:44–45, author's translation). Here, the limited-love principle is replaced with the unlimited love concept.

A similar challenge to the principle of limited love is found in the parable of the good Samaritan (Luke 10:25–37). In both these texts, Jesus taught that no one, especially those who claim to be citizens of God's kingdom, should ever respond to evil with evil. His *midrash* on that is, "Turn the other cheek." The final step in God's progressive teaching on retribution is that love, forgiveness, and justice must be applied equally to all humanity. One universal principle of justice must be applied to all people, regardless of their ethnicity, nationality, or religious faith.

As we discussed this section, Joseph Coleson observed[4] that this final principle of unlimited love is present already in the Pentateuch itself in God's statement, "Vengeance is Mine, and retribution" (Deut. 32:35 NASB). Jesus simply reminds us of this in his *midrash* in the Sermon on the Mount. This is an important observation, as it validates the thesis of this chapter that God's revelation and teachings, though necessarily bound by time and space, are still unchanging. In other words, the need for progressive revelation arises from human sinfulness—our inability to comprehend God's original and unchanging message. It is not, as some have argued, a proof that God's message to humanity is ever-evolving and changing through time and with the times.

GOD'S REVELATION AND CONTEMPORARY CHRISTIANITY

A key lesson this chapter is intended to teach is that the eternal and unchanging God who actively reveals himself in the pages of the Bible is neither a contradiction nor a "Christian invention." Some schooled in the scientific method can easily find the concept of progressive revelation within the pages of the Bible. However, they may also find it troubling and difficult to synchronize such findings with their understanding of the nature of God as unchanging and his revelation as unresponsive to human history. This chapter suggests progressive revelation is not only logical within human history, but is also consistent with a biblical understanding of God's nature. Moreover, God who reveals himself progressively, lures both Hebrew and Gentile into the future and into the divine, into the moment God will return once again to take his children home.

A derivative principle is that the progressive nature of God's story manifests itself daily in multiplied personal, living relationships with our Lord and Savior. John Wesley noted that Christian sanctification is a living, evolving process; in it, God's revelation is made present and real in the daily lives of God's followers, individually and communally. The progressive nature of revelation is visible in our need of a living, vertical relationship with God, for the establishment of relationships of full integrity with others who cross our paths, whether believers or unbelievers, friends or strangers. Only an anchored relationship with God, the ever-consistent and stable One, can bring genuine, permanent justice and love into the ever-shifting reality of human horizontal relationships.

A final call to believers is to ongoing serious and intentional learning, that we may know the whole of God's recorded revelation. This is necessary to avoid dangers such as situational theology, dogmatism, particularized morality, or misconceptions of history's *telos*— all these (and others) most often based on too narrow a selection of the Bible's total content. If we would take seriously God's progressive revelation, we must study, understand, and interpret the whole of God's recorded history and teachings. Only when we process the whole of God's revelation can we make sound and truthful doctrinal and theological pronouncements.

ACTION/REFLECTION SUGGESTIONS

1. In your own Bible study, whether personal or professional, begin looking for examples and patterns of the progressive nature of God's revelation.

2. As you discover these, ponder their implications for your understanding of God's relationship with his people, and for your own walk with Christ.

3. Consider: Could attention to and/or discussion of the progressive nature of God's revelation lead to positive changes in your beliefs about God's nature and attributes? With whom could you begin to study and discuss this important topic? How can you begin to incorporate what you learn into your preaching or teaching ministry?

FOR FURTHER READING

Bebbington, David. *Patterns in History: A Christian Perspective on Historical Thought.* Vancouver, B.C.: Regent College Publishing, 1990.

Bebbington has provided a useful tool for learning about non-Christian views of history. (This second edition of the book is now handled by Lightning Source Inc.)

Griffin, David R. *A Process Christology.* Philadelphia: The Westminster Press, 1973.

This is one of the earliest books to look at Christology using a "from below" model. As such, in addition to pointing out that Jesus is God's decisive self-revelation, it also provides a concise overview of God's self-revealing activities in human history.

Hallo, William W., and William Kelly Simpson. *The Ancient Near East: A History*. New York: Harcourt Brace Jovanovich, 1971.

This book is a very helpful aid to comprehending the historical and intellectual background of the Old Testament, with its excellent overview of ancient Mesopotamian and Egyptian understandings of history, as well as of their histories per se.

Jordan, Clarence. *Sermon on the Mount*. Valley Forge, Pa.: Judson Press, 1952.

One of my all-time favorite expositions of the Sermon on the Mount. Jordan, the founder of Koinonia Farm in Americus, Georgia, has done a brilliant job of showing the practicality of Jesus' words and teaching in and for everyday life.

Lewis, C. S. *Mere Christianity*. Available in numerous editions.

A powerful, logical defense of Christian faith and teaching, this most famous of Lewis's nonfiction works transcends denominational lines, discussing the many doctrines shared in common across the faith.

NOTES

1. For details of ancient Mesopotamian and Egyptian views of history, see William W. Hallo and William Kelly Simpson, *The Ancient Near East: A History* (New York: Harcourt Brace Jovanovich, 1971). David Bebbington, *Patterns in History: A Christian Perspective on Historical Thought* (Vancouver, B.C.: Regent College Publishing, 1990 [now handled by Lightning Source Inc.]), addresses the contrast between the Greek and the Hebrew/Jewish/New Testament views of history.

2. It's important to acknowledge a view of history dangerously similar to that presented by the Bible. Karl Marx also suggested human history is progressive, intentional, and moving to a predetermined end; Marx also said history is a record of the continuous transformation of humanity. Marx reached these conclusions based on his analysis of the world's history from an economic viewpoint, and argued for an unchanging, unstoppable historical momentum toward economic fairness and justice.

Serious students of history and theology concede similarities between the biblical and the Marxist views of history. Of course, the crucial difference is that the Bible identifies the eternal God, rather than temporal humans, as the "agent of change and progress." The Bible presents more than a record of human history; it's "God's history," the record of how God participates in, and thus reveals himself in, human history.

3. From Clarence Jordan, *Sermon on the Mount* (Valley Forge, Pa.: Judson Press, 1952); he discusses in some detail all four laws (murder, adultery, oath-taking, vengeance) upon which Jesus gave his *midrash*/commentary in the Sermon on the Mount (Matt. 5).

4. Joseph Coleson, private communication (e-mail), July 2, 2008.

PART 3

A WESLEYAN APPROACH TO INTERPRETING SCRIPTURE

11

LANGUAGE

David L. Thompson

*And whatever you do, in word or deed, do everything
in the name of the Lord Jesus, giving thanks to
God the Father through him.*

—Colossians 3:17 (NRSV)

O what a heavy curse was the confusion of tongues!

—John Wesley

Scriptural interpretation immerses the reader in human language issues. These range from understanding individual words to interpreting entire compositions and even literary corpuses, such as the biblical Pentateuch, or the Pauline Epistles. Careful study of language itself and of literary artifacts from the world of the Bible over the last century and a half has dramatically enhanced our ability to understand the meaning of scriptural texts at several points. Discerning the precise meanings of terms in context, describing the relationship of the parts of a composition to each other, and listening for the impact of a composition's social and/or historical context are among the points at which recent attention to language has raised the level of understanding open to modern readers of the Bible. In this chapter, as in most others in this book, we are concerned with language issues germane to the process of Scripture study, not simply Scripture reading.

LANGUAGE AND INTENTIONAL INTERPRETATION

If we read a text in a language we don't know, we may pronounce the words, but we will not understand the text. On the other hand, when we read a document in a language with which we have reasonable facility, we actually interpret the document as we read it. Reading such a document is interpreting it. Using the dictionaries, encyclopedias, histories, and other stores of information lodged in our minds in the process of learning the language, we interpret such a text immediately, intuitively. Depending on the extent of our mastery of the language of the text and the extent of our capacities to enter the thought-world of the text, our immediate, intuitive grasp of the text will be more or less complete and culture-bound.

If we wish to move beyond our immediate, intuitive grasp of the work to obtain a more complete, less culture-bound, more precise and adequate reading of the text, we will have to proceed to an intentional process of interpretation. This will involve asking questions regarding the meaning of the text and finding information within and beyond the text with which to answer our questions. In the process we will correct and extend our intuitive understanding by this more deliberate study of the text.

The larger the cultural gap between us and the world of the text, the more likely our intuitive grasp of the text will be incomplete, even skewed. Likewise, the more the vocabulary in the document falls outside our common stock of terms, the less likely our intuitive understanding is to be correct. Little wonder then that Christian

Scripture, coming to us from cultures foreign to us, far removed from us in time and space, and loaded with vocabulary unfamiliar to many modern readers, requires that we study the text just to make good sense of it. This intentional quest to interpret Scripture necessarily plunges us into language issues.

PLAYING BY THE RULES: LANGUAGE GAMES

Languages appear to work much like games. Each language is a different language game, played according to its own rules. The words of a given language have no essential relationship to the entities or concepts to which they refer. Rather, the relationship between a term and that to which it refers appears to be arbitrary, a matter of language convention and not of essential reality, philosophically considered. Thus, speakers of English have agreed to use the word *heart* to designate a central human organ, as well as select human capacities, spatial and conceptual locations, aspects of human character, and other matters. Those are the rules of the game. So long as users of the language "play" (i.e., speak and write) by its rules, they will communicate.

The game rules of each language are incredibly complex, even though native speakers learn the majority of them in childhood. They cover very detailed matters such as how the particular words are spelled, pronounced, and differentiated from related or similar terms. The language rules also cover general matters such as how the term can function along with others to compose a statement, question, directive, exclamation, or the like, and still more global rules such as how the statement will function with others to form a longer unit of thought like a simple or complex sentence, a paragraph, or a larger composition. Alternating attention to individual terms on the one hand and the contexts of which they are a part, on the other, eventually leads to increasing clarity in understanding both. One may begin with either pole in setting up the conversation between the whole and the parts.

All this is complicated in biblical study by the fact that most modern readers study Scripture in translation. Consequently three sets of language rules come into play simultaneously: (1) those of the modern language; (2) those of the translated biblical language—Hebrew, Aramaic, or Greek; and (3) those of human language in general. We can illustrate by the interpretation of Deuteronomy 6:5 in its various contexts.

Suppose that we want to understand Deuteronomy 6:5 because we've been directed to it by Jesus' citation of this text as "the greatest command." As recorded in the Gospels (e.g., Mark 12:30), Jesus quoted it, "Love the Lord your God with all your heart and with all your soul and with all your mind and with all your strength." Locating the Deuteronomy passage, we discover that, for reasons not immediately obvious, either Jesus or the gospel writers added "with all your mind" to the quotation. Deuteronomy 6:5 itself reads, "Love the LORD your God with all your heart and with all your soul and with all your strength." Although the sentence at first seems transparent, a bit of reflection raises numerous questions an uninformed reader would have to answer, to understand the quote in Mark as well as the passage in Deuteronomy. We are plunged into a process of intentional interpretation, in which we ask interpretive questions and answer them by careful attention to the clues to meaning within the text and its various contexts.

DISCOURSE CONTEXT: THE BOOK AS A WHOLE

Basically, we have to ask the meaning of each major element in the sentence: Who is the "you" being addressed? What do the terms *love*, *Lord*, *God*, *heart*, *soul*, and *strength*, and the repeated qualifier, "with all" mean here? To answer these questions, we need also to ask about the nature of the document in which our text resides, and its place in that document. Thus, we should begin our interpretive process by examining the literary context in which the text now stands, as the answers to these latter questions almost certainly will influence the answers to our earlier questions.

Reading backward and forward from our text, we discover that Deuteronomy 6:5 sits toward the beginning of a thirty-four chapter document. A brief opening paragraph identifies the book as "the words Moses spoke to all Israel" in the plains of Moab, as the people antici- pated their entry into the land God had promised them upon leaving Egypt (Deut. 1:1–5). It locates them chronologically as separated by forty years from the first Horeb (Sinai) events, which we know are narrated in the book of Exodus. It also refers to events narrated in the book of Numbers (the conquest of the Amorite kings). This introductory paragraph describes the content of the document as Moses' expounding of "this law" (1:5), versus a simple recitation or repetition, or a giving of the law. Moses' exposition of the Horeb law then begins with a review of the history of Israel from the revelation of God to Israel at Mount Horeb (1:6) to their location at Beth Peor (3:29). This historical review eventually includes Deuteronomy 1:6—4:43.

At Deuteronomy 4:44, the text changes direction, presenting actual commandments, though still housed in a narrative framework. This presentation of material described variously as commands, decrees, statutes, and ordinances continues on through chapter 26 and clearly comprises the bulk of the book (4:44—26:19). Moses related this material to the covenant the Lord had made with these people at Horeb (5:2–3), then began by recalling the core commands (the Ten Commandments, 5:6–21) given at Horeb for the gathered tribes, and reminding them of their situation at the time. Moses followed this basic covenantal law with exhortations regarding "this command- ment" (singular), beginning with our text (6:1–5). He exhorted them repeatedly to observe these commands carefully. Moses recalled bits of their history with the Lord aimed at supporting this obedience, and buttressed his exhortations with other motivations, as well.

At Deuteronomy 12, the writer announced, "These are the decrees and laws you must be careful to follow in the land that the LORD, the God of your fathers, has given you to possess" (12:1). This rubric introduces a section of more specific commands and exhortations running all the way to chapter 26 (i.e., 12:1—26:19). The upshot of this is that this major unit in the book appears itself to be comprised of two sections. The first chapters (4:44—11:32) give more general instruction (the ten commands and our text of 6:5) together with extensive instruction and theological grounding of this core law. Then chapters 12–26 contain more specific commands.

It actually appears that in the core Torah (4:44—11:32), Deuteronomy 6:5 serves as a definitive generalization of both the ten commands which precede it and the more specific commands that follow it in chapters 12–26. If this is so, then Deuteronomy presents "You shall love the LORD your God with all your heart and with all your soul and with all your strength" as a succinct conceptualization of Horeb law as expounded now by Moses. This loads it with heavy freight in and for the book as a whole. On the one hand, Deuteronomy 6:5 captures generally what all the book's exhortations aim at or constitute. On the other hand, the particulars of the book expound the concept of loving Yahweh with all the heart, soul, and strength.

Deuteronomy 27–29 state the consequences of keeping or not keeping these commands propounded by Moses on the plains of Moab, in terms of blessings and curses. Chapter 30 contains the hortatory culmination of the book, summarizing these alternative responses as the way of life and good, and the way of death and evil, respectively, climaxing in the exhortation, "Now choose life" (30:19). Chapter 29 refers to the content of Moses' exposition as a covenant God offered Moses' hearers in Moab, as well as all who read that Torah in the future (29:9, 12, 14–15). In doing so, it taps into the cross-temporal perspective the book generates by bringing the historic events at Horeb, the exposition by Moses in Moab, and unlimited future readings of the document in covenant renewals, into a single moment of response, "today" or "this day" (see 5:3; 27:1; 29:9–15).

The concluding chapters, Deuteronomy 31–34, (1) make provision for the reading of the Torah here expounded (31:9–13) and for its disposition (31:24 ff.); (2) designate witnesses to Moses' exposition of the law (31:19–22, 28; 32:1–47); (3) anticipate and narrate the death of Moses (31:1–2; 33:1–29; 34:1–5); and (4) provide for and narrate Joshua's orderly succession to leadership (31:7–8, 14, 23; 34:9). These chapters could strike us as a concluding catchall were it not for previous clues, especially those in 29:9–15, which relate Deuteronomy to ancient covenants/treaties.

LANGUAGE IN CULTURAL CONTEXT

We know enough about the content and literary structure of Hittite treaties/covenants of the second millennium B.C. and Neo-Assyrian treaties/covenants of the first millennium B.C. to conclude that Deuteronomy appears to have been structured by analogy with these ancient treaties. The book's historical prologue (1:6—4:43), the commands and ordinances (i.e., covenant stipulations, 4:44—26:19), the blessings and curses (27:1—30:20), and the provision for the covenant's recording, disposition, and promulgation with witnesses (chs. 31–33) all reflect the content and general order of these ancient suzerainty treaties.

These treaties structured the relationship between a dominant or conquering king (suzerain) and a subordinate king or ruler (vassal). Deuteronomy as it stands has been pressed into the service of warranting leadership in the line of Moses and Joshua and of defining legitimate Mosaic faith as faith in that tradition (cf. 1:1–6; 34:1–12). Even so, it still strongly evokes comparison with political treaties and suggests use in covenant renewal, making this aspect of the document's cultural context important to its understanding. Not every point of the analogy can be pressed, but several points of impact on the meaning of Deuteronomy 6:5 will emerge. The covenant/treaty form of Deuteronomy places the Lord in the role of the great King, here not a conqueror, but rather as a saving King. It places Israel in the position of those submitting as vassals, or as a collective "vassal," to the rule of the great King.

CULTURAL CONTEXT: LITERARY GENRE

Reference to treaties (i.e., covenants) raises the question of the literary genre of the book of Deuteronomy. The rules of our language game and those of the Bible, as well, demand attention to the general kind, or genre, of document before us. We know from English literary convention that different kinds of documents place different demands on readers and generate various expectations and interpretive strategies. For example, in North America we differentiate between a business letter, an informal letter, a personal note, a medical prescription, a mortgage, and a will. Each of these has a distinct form of presentation, different from the others. We read each with different assumptions and expectations for grammar, vocabulary, syntax, purpose, and meaning. Ancient biographies, histories, epistles, apocalyptic treatises, wisdom compilations—these are but a few of the literary genres readers of the Bible encounter.

The question of literary genre bears directly on our text. In ancient treaties of the sort noted earlier, the word *love* is a precise legal technical term. In treaty/covenant settings it means "to make and keep treaty" (i.e., a covenant). To love "with all the heart" means to keep covenant without reservation, without political duplicity or clandestine alliance with other kings. *Love* in this sense involves faithful service to the king and obedience to his directives. This is a "love" that can be commanded.

One can contrast the meaning of the term *love* here in Deuteronomy 6:5 with the use of the same term by the prophet Hosea. The differences are clear. In Hosea this word refers to the Lord's husband-like love of Israel, not to Israel's attitude toward God. Even though Hosea talked at length of covenant matters, he did not use the word *love* to describe Israel's relationship with God. Nor did he exhort Israel to love God. This is true even in chapter 2 where a future marriage of Israel to the Lord is envisioned.

Deuteronomy, on the other hand, does use the term *love* to describe covenantal relationships of Israel with the Lord. It has little if anything to do with romantic or familial love. God commands it and, as in secular treaties, "love" here carries assumptions of Israel's faithful service and obedience to God, the great King. The covenant-like genre of the book of Deuteronomy determines the sense of this word.

LANGUAGE GAMES AGAIN: GRAMMAR AND SYNTAX

Grammar is the study of the forms and structure of words and expressions that signal meaning in a given language. Syntax, a subset of grammar, concerns itself with the conventions by which words, phrases, and clauses are ordered and combined to produce meaningful utterances. In other words, grammar and syntax discern the "rules" of the language game by which an English reader makes sense of the text we have, but would struggle to make sense of Deuteronomy 6:5, if it ran like this: "Loves your shalls, you God LORD, heart all your with, all yours with and spirits, and and with you loves you might all!" None of this fits the rules of the English language game in form, structure, order, arrangement, or combination—i.e., in grammar and syntax.

Result? No meaningful communication. Our job now is to examine the language clues present in the great command that signal sense to us.

Keeping the treaty/covenant genre of the book as a whole in mind, we recall that Deuteronomy 6:5 sits in the "stipulations" section of the treaty/covenant document. Focusing on the sentence itself, we observe that in many translations (e.g., ESV, NKJV, NASB) the sentence begins with a single verb, "shall love," a subject, "you," and three qualifying prepositional phrases that appear to state the personal means by which the addressee is to love: "with (i.e., by means of) all your heart and with all your soul and with all your strength."

The Hebrew verb is future tense ("shall love"). It either simply makes a claim about the future, i.e., about what will be, or it carries hortatory force and thus stipulates the speaker's will about the future, what shall be the case. (In formal English, in the second and third persons, the auxiliary verb "shall" carries this hortatory sense—by contrast with "will love.") This forceful demand upon the future actually carries stronger hortatory force than a simple imperative would have done in this context. This construal is reinforced by the document's covenant genre connections, in which the imperative force would be at home.

But in the original language, the Deuteronomy 6:5 injunction actually begins with the conjunction "and," which ties our exhortation to preceding materials, at least to the lines in verse 4. Deuteronomy 6:4, we observe, is composed of an opening imperative with a noun of direct address, "Hear, O Israel!" followed by a claim apparently about the unity or "oneness" of Israel's God, Yahweh. As noted earlier, Deuteronomy 6:5 appears to serve as a definitive generalization of both the ten commands which precede it and the more specific commands that follow it in this stipulations section (chapters 12–26).

The coordination of the theological claim of verse 4 with the great command and the introductory focus on that command ("You shall love the LORD" ESV) in 6:1–3 imply that 6:4 may be as critical to the whole document as is 6:5. It may contain a "great confession" ("the LORD is one"), which, like the great command, is foundational for the entire book. It seems quite likely that the two verses are not simply coordinated, but that the great confession should be linked causally with the great command: "The LORD is one; *therefore*, you shall love the LORD . . ." (ESV, emphasis added).

Returning to the 6:5 stipulation as a whole, we must attend to grammatical details necessarily involved in language use. These grammatical signals are among the aspects of the text which on a first reading we interpret intuitively, but which we now examine more closely to test and expand our initial understanding. We've already noted the sentence is actually an injunction, by way of a verb that states the future emphatically—what "shall be" the case. Moreover, this call to "love" directs this covenant faithfulness to a specific object, "the Lord," a person further identified as "your God."

The introductions to many English Bible versions explain that "LORD," spelled with small caps, is a printing convention to signal the personal name of Israel's God, Yahweh, designated in the Hebrew consonantal text as YHWH. Examination of the larger literary corpus which Deuteronomy now concludes (Genesis–Deuteronomy) shows the object of the commanded covenant loyalty to be the God, Yahweh, who made himself uniquely known to Israel in his deliverance of them from Egypt (Ex. 6:1–3). This is the Yahweh who covenanted with them at the Mount to be their God, they to be his people (Ex. 19:4–6). The possessive pronoun that identifies this Lord as "your God" references this oath-bound relationship established by covenant at Sinai (Horeb). That covenant established the unique, enduring relationship between Israel and the Lord that is assumed, renewed, and expounded in Deuteronomy. It details the sense in which he "belongs" to them, and they to him.

Four additional matters of grammatical detail concern us. First, as noted earlier, three prepositional phrases modify the injunction by specifying the means by which one is to love the Lord—*with* or by means of your heart . . . your soul . . . your strength. Second, the adjective *all* qualifies each of the stated means by which one is to love the Lord—by means of one's *whole* heart, . . . one's *whole* soul, and . . . one's *full* strength, thus excluding a half-hearted, divided-soul, partial-strength response to the command. Third, the coordinating conjunction *and* links the three prepositional phrases together and at the same time separates them for individual note: "You shall love the LORD your God with all your heart, *and* with all your soul, *and* with all your strength" (ESV, emphasis added).

Fourth, all the second person pronominal references to *you* in the command are singular in number. This is not apparent in English, but the Hebrew text distinguishes *you* singular from *you* plural. This exhortation repeatedly addresses individuals: "*You* (sg.) shall love the Lord *your* (sg.) God with all *your* (sg.) heart, and with all *your* (sg.) soul, and with all *your* (sg.) strength" (ESV, emphasis added). This singular address presents a striking rhetorical move, given that the whole nation stood gathered on the plains of Moab (Deut. 1:1–6).

LANGUAGE AND WORD MEANINGS: LEXICOGRAPHY

We return now to the precise meanings of the terms of the great command. We attended earlier to the meaning of *love* in this context, nuanced by the covenantal or treaty genre analogy evoked by the whole book. We look now to the terms *heart, soul,* and *strength.* We keep in mind language insights referenced at the outset of the chapter, especially the insight that *use* is the most dependable indicator of a term's meaning. This means that if we want to know the meaning of the terms *heart, soul,* and *strength,* we should study all the biblical occurrences of the terms, beginning with their use in the book of Deuteronomy itself, proceeding to other literature influenced by Deuteronomy, then, eventually, to all occurrences of the terms in the Old Testament. We content ourselves here with illustrative occurrences of these words in Deuteronomy.

We observe that the occurrences in our target passage are not particularly informative regarding the meanings of the individual terms. That is, if we did not know the meanings of these terms as we came to this verse, and if this text were the only use of these terms we had, we would not learn much here about their meanings, and would not understand the statement itself much at all. We note that several of the occurrences of these terms in Deuteronomy are in repetitions or partial repetitions of the 6:5 command or the cluster of prepositional phrases (4:29; 10:12; 11:13, 18; 13:4; 26:16; 30:6, 10). These are apt to be no more informative than is our 6:5 occurrence.

We will look to other occurrences for more insight. In each case we will come to the occurrence asking something like this: "If this were the only occurrence we had of word X, what would we think it meant?" From 6:5 we would know that these three entities (heart, soul, strength) can be in some sense owned or possessed by the individual keeping covenant. We infer this because the one "loving" is to do so with all one's heart, one's soul, one's strength. Perhaps this means "heart," "soul," and "strength," are personal capacities or personal resources of the one keeping covenant.

"WITH ALL YOUR HEART"

A review of the occurrences of the two forms of the Hebrew word for *heart* shows the following data. In Deuteronomy the "heart" forgets (4:9) and in the process misunderstands the source of blessings (8:14–18). Positively, the "heart" understands and serves Yahweh (10:12–13). The "heart" is the place of self-talk, of reflection and mulling over matters

(7:17; 8:17; 9:4; 15:9; 18:21). The "heart" becomes over-confident, arrogant, and presumptuous (8:14, 17), and is open to deception (11:16). It becomes confused (28:28). The "heart" makes plans to obey or not to obey Yahweh's commands and internalizes Yahweh's word (11:18–21). The "heart" regrets (19:6) and is glad (28:47). The "heart" trembles and is afraid and intimidated (1:28; 20:8–9; 28:65), or on the other hand reverences and obeys the Lord (5:29).

Although this is not an exhaustive treatment, it's enough to indicate the main lines of data from Deuteronomy. The "heart" in Deuteronomy names the human faculty of thought, of cerebral matters. Planning, thinking, reflecting, evaluating, feeling, and committing are activities of the heart. The heart also houses attitudes and emotions. Expressions like "say in one's heart" seem semantically equivalent to "say to one's self" and appear to name the person from the perspective of thinking and feeling. The *mind*, it appears, would be a close synonym in modern English.

"WITH ALL YOUR SOUL"

Regarding the second term, *soul*, a review of its uses in Deuteronomy offers these findings. As can "heart," in Deuteronomy, "soul" can designate the self-identity of a person, hence "watch yourself" or "watch yourselves" (4:9, 15). "Soul" also designates the person, but more corporeally or fully considered: "seventy 'souls' went down to Egypt," i.e., "seventy people," viewed as individual, embodied persons who could be observed traveling or could be sold as slaves (10:22; 24:7; cf. 13:6). "Souls" in Deuteronomy internalize teaching (11:18); they languish (28:65). In Deuteronomy most frequently "souls" "desire" or "crave" food (12:15, 20, 21; 14:26; 23:24). They want to go certain places or enter certain conditions (18:6; 21:14). "Soul" designates the "life" as the "life force" or "animation" of persons (19:21), as associated with blood of animals (12:23). "Life for a life" (i.e., "soul for a soul") stipulates retaliation person for person, but considered as a living, embodied person (19:21). The "soul" focuses, prioritizes, and desires, as when one "seeks" Yahweh (4:29).

In the book of Deuteronomy, *soul* appears to designate persons as self-aware, living, thinking beings, as craving food and having other desires and preferences. Some overlap with the semantic domain of *heart* appears. But with *soul*, emphasis seems to fall on the person as a corporeal, embodied life. With this in mind, perhaps the most illuminating occurrence of this term appears in Genesis 2:7. There the Adam becomes a "living soul," i.e., a "living creature," carrying the same designation as the wildlife in chapter 1 (Gen. 1:20, 21, 24, 30), the "living creatures." *Soul* designates, then, not something persons have, but rather names what humans and animals are, living creatures with creaturely needs, desires, and identity.

"WITH ALL YOUR STRENGTH"

In the last of the three prepositional phrases, "with all your strength," we encounter an oddity. We expect the word translated *strength* or *might* in Deuteronomy 6:5 to function as a straightforward noun, controlled by the preposition *with*. The obvious parallel with the preceding two prepositional phrases—"with all your heart and with all your soul"—reinforces this expectation. But it functions nowhere else in the Old Testament as a noun, except in a repetition of our phrase in 2 Kings 23:25.

This term generally stands alone with adverbial force, meaning "much" or "very," or the like, variously translated, as in "multiply *greatly*" (6:3) or "*so* angry" (9:20) (emphasis added). It also appears in prepositional phrases like our own, but regularly with simple adverbial meaning, where the meaning of the noun as a noun is no longer clear. Examples of this adverbial use include Genesis 17:2, "multiply you *greatly*," and 17:6, "make you *exceedingly* fruitful" (both places, literally, "with strength, strength"; emphasis added).

The long and short of all this is that we do not have good, contextual information with which to determine the precise meaning of the noun usually translated *strength* here. Without adequately informative occurrences of our term to be sure of its meaning, we can turn to second level sources of information for getting at term meaning. We can appeal to etymology, linguistic cognates, and translational tradition.

Appeal to etymology, something of a desperation move, does not advance our understanding of this particular term. Reference to related terms in other Semitic languages locates an Ugaritic cognate meaning "abundance" and Akkadian cognates usually functioning as adjectives, "great" or "important." The pre-Christian Greek translation, the Septuagint (LXX), renders our word with "might" or "strength," as does Jerome's Vulgate. The ancient Aramaic translations take the term to mean "property" or "wealth." Our term illustrates well the difficulties of reaching certainty when occurrences of a term prove relatively uninformative. We will follow tradition and go with the earliest translators (LXX), under the assumption that they knew more about the term's meaning than we may.

A COMPREHENSIVE PARAPHRASE

We can summarize our findings in the form of a paraphrasing translation, guided by the rules of the language games which surface in Deuteronomy 6:4–5:

Pay attention, O Israel, God's people since the mount! Because of Yahweh's fundamental unity, therefore you—each of you— shall keep covenant with Yahweh, your God, in thoroughgoing integrity, without a hint of duplicity or alien allegiance. And you will fully engage your critical, mental capacities, your whole personal, creaturely identity, and your entire accumulated clout in serving Yahweh. This faithful covenant loyalty is at issue in your observance of each of the Ten Core Commands, on the one hand, and also in your honest compliance with each of the many specific statutes and ordinances with which Moses expounded the Great Command, on the other.

Our interpretive efforts have been aimed, finally, at simply discerning the plain sense of the text as an ideal first reader of Deuteronomy might have understood it. A more complete interpretation of the text would have us discerning ways in which this command, as we have interpreted it, colors our understanding of the book of Deuteronomy itself. A full interpretation would lead us to reflect on the assumptions that lie behind this command and to pursue insights that can be inferred from the text. In the process we would surely learn more about the theology entailed in Deuteronomy 6:5, about the ethics and morality of the command, and much more.

With this reading of Deuteronomy 6:4–5, we return to Jesus' quotation in Mark 12:30, and the question of the meaning of that quotation in its context with which we began. The interpretation of Mark 12:30, itself, will engage the same language issues tied to Deuteronomy 6:5. Beyond his quotation of the great command, one wonders whether Jesus' instruction that connects loving him with keeping his commandments (John 14:15 and related texts) might not trade in the language of the Deuteronomic covenant tradition. Treating Jesus' and then Mark's quotation itself will broach hermeneutical issues such as intertextuality and canonical reading, questions beyond the scope of this chapter.

ACTION/REFLECTION SUGGESTIONS

1. Locate a favorite passage of Scripture. Examine it with your English grammar glasses on. Note all the places where discerning the text's grammatical features enhances your reading of it, even in translation.

2. Think of the different literary genres you know about—e.g., epistles, songs, historical narratives, biographies, prophetic speeches. Suggest some implications of God's use of such language tools for revealing himself.

3. To understand the cost incurred from not knowing much about the cultural and historical contexts of Scripture, contemplate the confusion you would have if you thought Henry VIII, Abraham Lincoln, and Colin Powell were contemporaries, the way some readers proceed as though David, Isaiah, and Nehemiah were contemporaries.

4. Study Mark 2:1—3:6. Note how Mark structured this narrative by presenting five episodes (2:1–12, 13–17, 18–22, 23–28; and 3:1–6) with remarkably parallel development. See if you can discern the parallel layout of this unit and the result it has for focusing a reader's attention on issues apparently of concern to Mark.

FOR FURTHER READING

Arnold, Bill T., and John H. Choi. *A Guide to Biblical Hebrew Syntax.* Cambridge: Cambridge University Press, 2003; Wallace, Daniel B. *Greek Grammar Beyond the Basics.* Grand Rapids: Zondervan, 1996.

These two grammars of the chief biblical languages present the next best step, after working with linguistic or language issues in English, in learning the "language games" most pertinent to careful interpretation of the biblical text. Focusing on syntax, they're not concerned with teaching basic paradigms, forms, and rules of combination, but rather with probing their meanings. Even the English-only reader will benefit from the help of these texts in getting into language issues in biblical interpretation.

Cotterell, Peter, and Max Turner. *Linguistics and Biblical Interpretation*. Downers Grove, Ill.: InterVarsity Press, 1989.

Cotterell and Turner present the major language issues involved in biblical interpretation in clear and understandable terms. Discerning word meanings and the literary structures of compositions large and small receive particularly fine treatment.

Grant, Robert M., with David Tracy. *A Short History of the Interpretation of the Bible*, 2nd edition. Philadelphia: The Fortress Press, 1984.

Grant, especially, has one of the best surveys available of the church's reading of Scripture. Tracy's survey of modern interpretive strategies is also useful. I have found this volume particularly helpful in understanding the various hermeneutical issues a modern Christian interpreter of the Bible has to take into account, and also for locating my hermeneutical and exegetical method within the tradition of the church.

GOLD INTO PYRITE, MOSTLY

Various Authors

And they read from the book, from the Torah—
the instruction—of God, interpreting it. And they gave
the sense, so the people understood the reading.

—Nehemiah 8:8 (editor's translation)

I have spent my life learning to read [the Scripture],
and teaching others to read.

—Gerhard von Rad

T his final chapter is a collection of discrete examples intended to illustrate hermeneutical and exegetical principles discussed throughout the book. In the nature of the case, most will be negative examples needing correction, but that is by no means a bad thing. Often, we can get to what something is more quickly by learning what it is not. If you were familiar with American sports, but had never seen or heard of cricket, and I told you, "It's more like baseball than football," you would recognize your first cricket match. You'd see immediately that cricket is nothing like American football, but does resemble baseball in several respects.

Positive or negative, these examples are illuminating and (mostly) fun to read. Enjoy!

DID NAHUM PREDICT THE AUTOMOBILE?

Nahum 2:4 reads: "The chariots storm through the streets, rushing back and forth through the squares. They look like flaming torches; they dart about like lightning."

An internet search yields hundreds of hits where this verse is interpreted as a prophetic prediction of the invention of the automobile, considered one of the heralds of the end times. But that interpretation violates the principle that an Old Testament prophecy must be understood first in its original literary and historical contexts. Only by removing this verse entirely from those contexts, and reading it totally through a contemporary lens, could a reference to chariots be construed as a reference to automobiles.

The literary context of the verse is Nahum 2, a prophecy against Nineveh, the Assyrian capital. Its historical context is the 600s B.C. The oracle is predictive prophecy, but it foretold the end of the Assyrian empire, the dominant power in the Middle East at that time. Nahum described an enemy capturing and plundering Nineveh. Thus, verse 4 is a poetic description of enemy chariots racing through Nineveh's streets during the battle. Nahum's prophecy was fulfilled literally in its historical context; the Babylonians captured Nineveh in 612 B.C., as God had forewarned through Nahum's oracle.

Does Nahum 2:4 predict automobiles with headlights ("flaming torches") filling modern streets and thoroughfares? Only if one deliberately divorces the verse from its literary and historical settings, and suppresses the fact that Nahum's prediction was fulfilled long ago. Sometimes chariots are nothing more than chariots.

—*KF**

UNDER HER WINGS

One of Jesus' most emotional pronouncements derives its intense power from his use of a vivid mother metaphor, portraying a small domestic scene many of Jesus' hearers would have seen often in their own courtyards: "O Jerusalem, Jerusalem, . . . how often I have longed to gather your children together, as a hen gathers her chicks under her wings, but you were not willing!" (Luke 13:34).

Our best-loved psalm employs a similarly familiar image throughout: "The LORD is my shepherd, . . . I will fear no evil, for you are with me; . . . I will dwell in the house of the LORD forever" (Ps. 23: 1, 4, 6). John the Baptist proclaimed Jesus "the Lamb of God" (John 1:29). The characteristics and the care of animals in the biblical world is a fascinating study, whether the specific passage or verse that prompts you to it is a literal or a figurative reference.

—JC

USAGE MATTERS

Some issues don't quite qualify as "hermeneutics," yet they add to or subtract from the confidence others will have in us as interpreters. For example, refer to Psalm 1, not Psalm*s* 1. Announce the Scripture as Revelation 4, not Revelation*s* 4. Years ago, a fellow Old Testament scholar told me of hearing a sermon on the "scrapegoat." One slip, even uncorrected, would not have posed a problem, but the preacher's mispronouncing the key word throughout the sermon did not inspire confidence in his knowledge of the *scapegoat* and its significance in Leviticus 16.

—JC

A WISDOM SAYING OR A PROMISE?

Proverbs 22:6 reads: "Start children off on the way they should go, and even when they are old they will not turn from it" (TNIV).

Some Christian parents, with grown children who are not walking with Christ, take this verse as a source of hope that the wanderer eventually will return to faith because of childhood training. It evokes feelings of condemnation in other Christian parents; they must have failed as parents, or their grown child would not have strayed from the faith, with no sign of returning. What these perspectives have in common is taking the second part of the proverb as an inevitable result or a divine promise, since it is a biblical proverb.

However, a proverb is not a guarantee. Its result statement is a general rule, with the understanding that exceptions occur. We recognize this more readily, perhaps, with non-biblical proverbs. Generally, "An apple a day keeps the doctor away." But healthy eating does not guarantee one never will have to see a physician. "Early to bed, early to rise, makes a person healthy, wealthy, and wise" is a truism, but some people acquire wealth by burning the candle at both ends.

A proverb's occurrence in the Bible does not transform it into something other than a proverb. We interpret even biblical proverbs by the rules of the "proverb" genre. One rule is that we are not to take result statements as inevitabilities.

Is Proverbs 22:6 a divine promise that a wayward child inevitably will return to a Christian upbringing? No. Does it accuse such a child's parents of bad parenting? No. Freedom of choice also is a consideration. Generally, children raised in Christian homes do continue in the faith—but not always. Some who wander never return to faith, either, but this does not invalidate the truthfulness of the proverb.

—KF

THE GATE THAT WASN'T

Matthew 19:24 and Mark 10:25 record Jesus' piquant observation that it's easier for a camel to go through the eye of a needle than for a rich person to enter the kingdom of God. It wouldn't be difficult to find the "explanation" that "the Eye of the Needle" was the popular nickname of the smallest of Jerusalem's gates at that time. Some go further, adding that a camel could enter that gate, but only by having its burden offloaded, and getting on its knees. Think of the applications; that will preach!

Unfortunately for our "applications," this is fabrication from beginning to end. Small gates, called posterns, were features of some ancient city walls, but Jerusalem needed none, and there are no records of postern gates in Herod's Jerusalem. Moreover, a camel on its knees could not make its way through any gate, large or small. The camel, the largest domestic animal of ancient Judea, could not squeeze through the tiny eye of the smallest domestic tool—it's as simple as that. Jesus was using the common literary device of hyperbole, exaggeration for effect.

—JC

NO TO YES, AND YES TO NO

Ancient Israel was forbidden to eat pork, rabbit, and shellfish, among other things. They could not weave together different materials, such as linen with cotton, or linen with wool. They were not to sell a field permanently; women who inherited land were not to marry outside their tribes. Most Christians today would not think of any of these things in moral or ethical terms. We eat what we want, mostly; we wear fabric of mixed materials; we buy and sell; we marry whom we please (in two senses of that word, at least!).

Conversely, ancient Israelites could buy, sell, and hold other humans in slavery. Men were permitted multiple wives, concubines, and even servant girls to whom they had sexual access. One responsibility of the kinsman-redeemer (*go'el*) was to execute, if he could, one who had killed his relative, even if accidentally, as long as the manslayer had not reached a city of refuge. Israelites were to offer several animal sacrifices each year if they could afford it. Today, the Christian who did any of the first three acts in this paragraph would acknowledge himself a sinner;

anyone doing them would be convicted as a criminal in most of the world today. The Christian who offered animal sacrifices would be counted immature and misinformed, at best.

Why does the Bible teach "no to yes" on some things, and "yes to no" on others? The cases are different, but they have in common the progressiveness of God's redemptive dealing with humanity. The reality of holiness—relationships of integrity with God and God's people—is constant; its particularized expressions across time, and from culture to culture, may change. Moreover, though perhaps God could mature us instantly, he simply doesn't work that way. God works with his people, through time and through lifetimes. Some things permitted never were *holy*, and we have learned that. Some things previously necessary to holiness have been brought to fulfillment in Christ, and now are, or may be, discretionary.

—JC

PHYSICS, POETRY, OR BOTH?

Read this quotation from a physics textbook, and consider how you would interpret it when you have it defined for you as scientific writing: "And hence no force, however great, can draw a cord, however fine, into a horizontal line which shall be absolutely straight" (from William Whewell, *Elementary Treatise on Mechanics*, 1819). Is this language to be taken literally? What do I look for? Other questions will occur to you.

Now read the same lines as poetry, and bring to bear issues important to the reading and interpretation of poetry—rhyme, meter, imagery, etc.:

And hence no force, however great,
Can draw a cord, however fine,
Into a horizontal line
Which shall be absolutely straight.

Having considered the difference between the same words read first as a scientific proposition, then as a poetic statement, ask yourself: Will similar differences be reflected in our reading of biblical narrative, in contrast to our reading of biblical poetry? Does, or should, the genre of a passage determine its factual accuracy? Its truth value?

—KF

THE SHELTER

The sermon title, "A Shelter in the Time of Storm," was inviting, as I was encountering significant stress in my life. The text, from Genesis 6, comprised God's directives to Noah for constructing an ark. The central point was that we can look to Jesus as our refuge in the difficult passages of life—well and good. But note some of the comparisons used to make that point:

1. The ark was made of wood but covered with tar, just as Jesus was divine but cloaked in humanity. I wondered whether some ancient heresy about the two natures of Christ might be resurrected in that analogy.

2. Just as the ark had a door, so Jesus is the door to heaven. The door was on the side of the ark, revealing Jesus' access to humanity. The window in the ark looked heavenward, indicating Jesus' relationship with God.

3. When the storm came, the ark was lifted up and floated on the water. Even so, the Master, lifted up on the cross, was suspended between earth and sky to bring us salvation. That had parallels with the serpent in the wilderness (John 3:14); I was left wondering whether every instance of something being off the ground had reference to Jesus.

There were other allusions: to the water, to the dove, to the mountain on which the ark came to rest. I had to admit the sermon was a well-crafted allegory, but the straining for all possible connections between boat and benefactor left me puzzled and bemused.

—CB

THE BRAMBLE KING

Before continuing here, read Judges 9, noting especially Jotham's parable. It has one point: Jotham's half-brother Abimelech was not fit to rule Israel—in fact, he would destroy those who trusted in him. Not long after the 1988 U. S. presidential election, I tried to make the point in an Old Testament survey course that most parables have only one major point; to expand them is misleading and counterproductive. I offered the most ridiculous allegorizing of Jotham's parable I could come up with: Greece has many olive trees; Michael Dukakis, the Democratic nominee in 1988, is Greek, ethnically; therefore, the olive tree in Jotham's parable from about 1100 B.C. represents Michael Dukakis. Nearly half the class thought I was serious!

Allegorical interpretation is not wrong; Paul and much of the early church used it. However, allegorizing tends to suppress the more important understandings of any passage allegorized. Secondly, you and I are not Paul. We do not have the Holy Spirit's inspiration for writing Scripture as Paul did, and his allegorizing is but a small part of his interpretation of a few earlier Scripture passages. Our allegorical interpretation will be obvious spiritualizing of the text, or it will be deceptive misrepresentation. The former is nearly valueless; the latter usually is dangerous. Use New Testament allegorizing where you find it, but please don't invent your own. It may be as ridiculous as mine was, intentionally, but someone is bound to take it seriously!

—JC

AN ADVENT REVERSAL

Second Sunday of Advent. On the screen, a song I'd never encountered: "While We Are Waiting, Come." A nice little tune, but as we sang the line the first time, the inevitable thought for a student of biblical history and theology was, "It should be, 'While He is coming, wait!'" We do not command God to come to us at our convenience. Even if we sing it as an invitation instead of a command, Advent is the season for us to practice waiting, to reflect upon Jesus' first Advent, and learn how to wait expectantly for his return, his second Advent.

If it's important enough to compose, it's important enough to get it right. If you are responsible for worship content, hold composers and lyricists accountable for what they put on paper. The biblical, theological, and musical appropriateness of music and lyrics is your concern. Hermeneutics may begin with Scripture; but it doesn't end there.

—JC

WHEN "VISION" MEANS "REVELATION"

When churches and other Christian organizations write or revisit mission statements, they often quote Proverbs 29:18, "Where there is no vision, the people perish" (KJV). Most often in that context, they understand "vision" as goal setting or imagining the big picture for the future. Thus, they interpret the verse as saying that when a Christian organization does not have a plan for growth and outreach, it ends up in disarray and goes nowhere.

This example illustrates the need for accurate contextual understanding of the English words used to translate the biblical languages. As in most languages, an English word often carries several different meanings and connotations, and we need to be sure we use the correct English definition for the term in the biblical passage. English *vision* carries at least three different meanings: (1) "sight," the ability to see something with the eye; (2) "the power of imagination" to dream big about the future—as in the kinds of settings noted above; and (3) "a special revelation from God," like those of prophetic visions in the Old Testament.

The issue becomes, then, which definition is correct in this verse? One way to find out is to do a word study of the Hebrew word. But what if one doesn't know Hebrew or Greek (for New Testament word studies)? One method that usually works is to compare English translations. For this verse, we see NIV and NKJV have "Where there is no revelation"; NLT, "When people do not accept divine guidance"; and ESV, "Where there is no prophetic vision." By comparing with other translations, it becomes obvious that the appropriate definition of KJV's "vision" here is number three, a divine revelation, rather than number two, the imaginings of one's own heart. The point of the verse is the necessity of guidance and instruction from God. In Old Testament times, this often came through the prophets; it comes to us primarily through Scripture.

Possessing now the appropriate definition, we need to remember, too, that prophetic "visions" in the Old Testament were not primarily revelations about divine intent for the future. They were calls for repentance, exhortations to be faithful to God, and encouragement in desperate times. When Proverbs 29:18 speaks of "vision," we should hear "divine revelation," and understand it as involving more than just a future perspective (though it can include that). It refers primarily to the word God would be speaking to the current condition of God's people.

This is confirmed by the pairing of *torah* (instruction/law) in the parallel line (29:18) as synonymous with "vision" of the first line: "but he that keepeth the law, happy is he" (KJV). Here, to take "vision" as the "vision casting" of a group is to misinterpret the verse.

—*KF*

"WOMEN SHOULD REMAIN SILENT"

First Corinthians 14:34–35 is often used to deny women leadership in the church. Yet to make these verses a universal mandate is to make Paul deny himself. Paul worked with women; he penned Galatians 3:28, the paradigm statement on all these matters; he called Junia an apostle (Rom. 16:7), though many English versions disguise this fact, without warrant making the name masculine, Junias. Even in this letter, Paul spoke just three chapters earlier (1 Cor. 11:5) of women praying and prophesying—public worship functions in the first century church—as though this were routine. If texts mean anything, these two verses cannot be universal commands.

What are they, then? Verse 35 is the answer, ". . . they should ask . . . at home." Most women were uneducated. Families did not sit together during worship. Some women believers in Corinth had fallen into the habit of calling out questions to their husbands when they heard something they didn't understand. In these verses, Paul was counseling these women to stop disrupting worship, have patience, and ask their husbands at home. He was not forbidding all women everywhere, in every time, to speak in Christian worship.

First Timothy 2:11–15 is often misread and misinterpreted in the same way. The issues in this passage are a bit more complex, and include even correcting an ancient mistranslation. But correct understanding of the entire paragraph leads to the same conclusion. Paul did not contradict himself here, either, but was concerned to stop some Ephesian women from teaching heresy in the churches of Ephesus. (Check the websites of Wesleyan Holiness Women Clergy, www.whwomenclergy.org, and Christians for Biblical Equality, www.cbeinternational.org, for many more resources on these and other related issues.)

—JC

"IF MY PEOPLE . . ."

At various days of prayer, or when talking about how revival will come to North America, leaders often quote 2 Chronicles 7:14, "If my people, who are called by my name, will humble themselves and pray and seek my face and turn from their wicked ways, then will I hear from heaven and will forgive their sin and will heal their land." They take this verse as a divine promise that when the followers of Christ ("my people") do these things, God will bring spiritual healing to the nation (U.S., Canada, or another country) in which they live ("their land").

We can affirm the continuing relevance of this Old Testament verse for the New Testament church. Still, we need to recognize differences between the two contexts, if we would understand and use it properly in the newer context.

In the Old Testament context, "my people" was Israel, God's covenant partner. In the New Testament context, it's appropriate to take the verse as now including both Jewish and Gentile followers of Christ. Accurate understanding, however, requires that we similarly expand the concept of "the land," rather than take it as referring still to a geopolitical entity, especially if that "land" is not Israel. The New Testament broadens the concept of "land," applying it to the kingdom of God or to the church (e.g., Gal. 4:26; Heb. 11:13–16). An appropriate transference is that if the followers of Christ pray and humble themselves, God will hear and heal the church. Of course, when the church truly seeks God and receives God's healing, this affects nation(s) where God's people live, but this verse addresses God's dealings with God's people—national Israel of the Old Testament, the followers of Jesus in the New Testament.

—*KF*

SHADDAI

Most English versions translate Hebrew *Shaddai*, "Almighty"; this is incorrect. That's a strong statement, but many Old Testament scholars agree (cf. the extended entry in *TDOT*), though there is little agreement anymore on what this divine title does mean.

Here an accurate etymology helps, because it works in the right direction. Several have been proposed. The translation "Almighty" reflects a presumed derivation from Akkadian *shadu*, "mountain," but a biblical Hebrew connection with Akkadian *shadu* is tenuous, and otherwise unattested. Moreover, Hebrew has two other common nouns meaning "mountain" or "height."

Biblical Hebrew itself attests only two possible roots. Some have advanced *shdd*, "ruin," "devastate," as the root of *Shaddai*, but there is neither semantic nor theological warrant for that in its Hebrew Bible usage.

The noun *shod*, "breast," from *shdh*, occurs twenty-four times in the Hebrew Bible, and *Shaddai*, just under fifty times. Translators, ancient and modern, have shied away from this root for obvious reasons, but have been victimized by false modesty and an implicit semi-Gnostic theology. Close consideration of the usage of *Shaddai* across its range yields the plausible and credible understanding, "the breasted one." This is the most important of several feminine characterizations of God, complementing the much more frequent masculine characterizations, and reminding us that God is not conceived as one-gendered, masculine only, as too much of our conscious thought and subconscious imaging takes for granted. Because God is not (only) masculine, both female and male are created in God's image (Gen. 1:27).

When your English translation reads "Almighty" or "God Almighty" (*El Shaddai*), use instead a full-orbed paraphrasing translation that reflects *Shaddai* more accurately: "The Breasted One, i.e., God who provides every need, as the nursing mother provides every need of the nursing infant." This is neither modernist nor feminist theology, but biblical translation of integrity, using all the tools at our disposal, and revealing to us the tender side of God needed by, and available to, all God's people, men, women, and children alike.

KF – *Kelvin Friebel*; *CB* – *Clarence Bence*; *JC* – *Joseph Coleson*

ABOUT
THE AUTHORS

CLARENCE BENCE (most friends call him "Bud") is Vice President and Academic Dean for the College of Arts and Sciences at Indiana Wesleyan University. Bud spent his childhood in upstate New York, where his father was a pastor and district superintendent in The Wesleyan Church. After studies at Houghton College and Asbury Seminary, Bud became pastor of the Penfield, New York, Wesleyan Church, where he developed a large youth program and a congregation open to the "Jesus Movement" of the early 1970s. After five years in Penfield, he enrolled in the doctoral program at Emory University, and earned a Ph.D. in Wesley Studies.

For the past twenty-five years, Dr. Bence has devoted himself to teaching in Wesleyan colleges—first at United Wesleyan College, then at Indiana Wesleyan University (formerly Marion College). In addition to his ministry in the classroom, he has served as Academic Dean at both Houghton College and Indiana Wesleyan University. He has authored a commentary on the book of Romans in a multi-volume series produced by Wesleyan Publishing House, and was one of the editors of the *Reflecting God Study Bible*.

Bud is married to Carol, who is Director of Nursing Programs in Indiana Wesleyan University's College of Adult and Professional Studies. The Bences have three grown children.

ELAINE BERNIUS is assistant professor of Biblical Studies at Indiana Wesleyan University in Marion, Ind. where she enjoys mentoring, teaching classes in biblical literature and languages, and having coffee with both students and colleagues. She holds a BA degree in Classical and Biblical Languages from Asbury College, and an M.Phil. in Hebraic and Cognate Studies from Hebrew Union College-Jewish Institute of Religion in Cincinnati, Ohio. This institution is also her current home for her dissertation work in Comparative Semitic Linguistics. Elaine is an ordained deacon in the Church of the Nazarene.

Elaine is blessed with a wonderful husband, Brian, who also teaches in the Division of Religion and Philosophy at Indiana Wesleyan. They have two children. Todd Matthew is a four-year-old bundle of energy who loves preschool, big trucks, and eating in the cafeteria at IWU. Asher Elizabeth is a very happy, contented baby, just beginning to explore her world. A yellow lab mix named Boaz completes their family.

CHRISTOPHER T. BOUNDS is associate professor of Theology at Indiana Wesleyan University. He earned a BA degree in Bible/Greek from Asbury College, and an M.Div. from Asbury Theological Seminary. His M.Phil. and Ph.D. degrees, both in Systematic Theology/Wesleyan Theology, are from Drew University. Dr. Bounds has published scholarly articles in *The Wesleyan Theological Journal, The Asbury Theological Journal, Studia Patristica, The Expository Times,* and *Religious Studies Review,* and is finishing a book, *The Doctrine of Christian Perfection in the Ante-Nicene Fathers,* to be published by Scarecrow Press.

Dr. Bounds is an ordained elder in The Arkansas Conference of The United Methodist Church, where he served as an associate and senior pastor for eight years before coming to Indiana Wesleyan University. Presently, he leads in a liturgical worship venue for College Wesleyan Church in Marion, Ind.

Chris and his wife, Tamara, have two children, a daughter Maris, and a son Morgan; as a family, they enjoy visiting museums and zoos. Chris is also a college football fan (Notre Dame Fighting Irish) and enjoys following high school football and basketball in the state of Indiana.

GARETH LEE COCKERILL was ordained a minister in The Wesleyan Church in 1969; he is a member of the Shenandoah District. Dr. Cockerill is professor of New Testament and Biblical Theology at Wesley Biblical Seminary, Jackson, Miss. He earned a BA degree from Southern Wesleyan University, an M.Div. from Asbury Theological Seminary, and Th.M. and Ph.D. degrees from Union Theological Seminary, Richmond, Virginia. Dr. Cockerill is writing a commentary on Hebrews to be published by Eerdmans in the New International Commentary on the New Testament.

Dr. Cockerill and his wife, Rosa, served for nine years as missionaries in Sierra Leone, West Africa, where they were engaged in evangelism, teaching, administration, and medical ministries. The Cockerills have three adult daughters, two sons-in-law, one grandson, and one granddaughter.

JOSEPH COLESON is a native of western Michigan. His BA is from Indiana Wesleyan University, his MA and Ph.D. degrees from Brandeis University. Since 1995, he has been professor of Old Testament at Nazarene Theological Seminary, and an adjunct professor at the University of Missouri, Kansas City. He is a Fellow of the Wesley Studies Centre, University of Manchester, England. Previously, he served on the faculties of Roberts Wesleyan College and Western Evangelical Seminary. Dr. Coleson is ordained in The Wesleyan Church; his pastoral experience is in two Conferences of the United Methodist Church.

Dr. Coleson is editor of this series, *Wesleyan Theological Perspectives*. He recently finished a commentary on Joshua for the *Cornerstone Biblical Commentary* (Tyndale), and is working on Genesis for the *New Beacon Bible Commentary* from Beacon Hill Press. He is a frequent contributor to adult Christian education curricula.

Dr. Coleson enjoys family life with his wife, Charlotte, a retired elementary-education reading specialist, and time with their two grown children and their spouses, and with two lively grandchildren. Reading mystery novels and gardening are two of his other interests.

KELVIN FRIEBEL is associate professor of Old Testament at Houghton College. He is ordained in The Wesleyan Church, and was a pastor for more than eight years in the Wisconsin District. He earned a BA degree from Seattle Pacific University, and both MA and Ph.D. degrees in Hebrew and Semitic Studies from the University of Wisconsin-Madison. His primary area of Old Testament research is in the books of Jeremiah and Ezekiel.

Kelvin and his wife, Margaret, lived in Regina, SK, for sixteen years, where he taught at Canadian Theological Seminary (now Ambrose University College). During that time, he also served as interim pastor at three different churches, and as an adjunct professor at two Bible colleges. Prior to Kelvin and Margaret's moving back to the U.S. in 2006, all the Friebel family had become dual U.S. and Canadian citizens; their two grown and married children live in western Canada.

In pursuit of his passion for teaching the Old Testament and its relevance to the church today, Kelvin has taught and preached overseas, in Hong Kong, Jordan, Lebanon, Nicaragua, Thailand, and the Philippines, besides teaching at Bethany Bible College in New Brunswick.

D. DAREK JARMOLA is a third-generation, Polish-born evangelical from the Baptist-Pentecostal-Methodist tradition. He earned a BD degree from International Baptist Theological Seminary, and a Ph.D. in Historical Theology/Reformation Studies from Southern Baptist Theological Seminary. He also holds an MBA (Marketing and Human Resources) from Oklahoma Wesleyan University (OWU).

Since 1994, Dr. Jarmola has served at OWU in a variety of positions: as soccer coach, Director of International Programs, as well as the Dean and Vice President for Adult and Graduate Studies. He now serves as professor of Historical Theology and Director of the Persecuted Church Ministries program. Dr. Jarmola is a regular contributor to the *Sixteenth Century Journal*.

Dr. Jarmola is an avid traveler, having been to more than thirty countries on four continents. He is married to Denise, a part-time instructor of stage craft who also directs theater productions at OWU. They have two children, a son, Darku, and a daughter, Kasia.

STEPHEN J. LENNOX has taught Bible and related subjects at Indiana Wesleyan University since 1993. Prior to that time, he pastored several Wesleyan churches. He earned a BA degree from Houghton College, an M.Div. from Evangelical Theological Seminary, and both an M.Phil. and a Ph.D. from Drew University.

Dr. Lennox has written two commentaries, *Psalms: A Bible Commentary in the Wesleyan Tradition*, and *Proverbs: A Bible Commentary in the Wesleyan Tradition*, both published by Wesleyan Publishing House. He is the author of *God With Us: An Introduction to the Old Testament*, published by Triangle Publishing, and of numerous articles. He has served as an editor of *Religious and Theological Abstracts* for more than fifteen years.

Dr. Lennox is married to Eileen; they have two grown children. They love to read and travel; their destinations have included Turkey,

Greece, Russia, the British Isles, and a number of countries in the Middle East.

KENNETH SCHENCK is professor of Religion at Indiana Wesleyan University where he teaches New Testament and Philosophy. He earned an AB degree in Religion from Southern Wesleyan University, an M.Div. from Asbury Theological Seminary, an MA in Classical Languages and Literature from the University of Kentucky, and a Ph.D. in New Testament from the University of Durham, England. He was ordained in the Florida District of The Wesleyan Church in 1991.

Dr. Schenck is an established author with more than half a dozen books published. His most recent are *Cosmology and Eschatology in Hebrews* (Cambridge University Press, 2007), and a second edition of *A Brief Guide to Biblical Interpretation* (Triangle Publishing, 2008).

Dr. Schenck and his wife, Angela, have four children, Stefanie, Stacy, Thomas, and Sophia. When deadlines aren't suffocating him, he likes to jog.

DAVID L. THOMPSON is F.M. and Ada Thompson Professor of Biblical Studies at Asbury Theological Seminary, and an ordained elder in the Kentucky District of The Wesleyan Church. He holds an AB degree from Indiana Wesleyan University, a BD and a Th.M. from Asbury Theological Seminary, and a Ph.D. in Ancient Near Eastern Studies from Johns Hopkins University. Dr. Thompson taught biblical studies at United Wesleyan College and Indiana Wesleyan University before going to Asbury in 1976. From 1982 to 1986, Dr. Thompson was pastor of Aspen Hill Wesleyan Church, Rockville, Md.; he also served as Minister of Worship and Pastoral Care at Stonewall Wesleyan Church, Lexington, Ky., 1994 to 1998.

Dr. Thompson's most recent book, *God's Healing for Hurting Families* (Wesleyan Publishing House), is based on the book of

Ephesians. It explores Christian holiness in light of recent recovery and family systems insights. His publications include *Bible Study That Works* (Evangel Press), and *Study Guide for J. Gresham Machen's New Testament Greek for Beginners* (Macmillan), as well as various scholarly and popular articles for the church and the academy.

Dr. Thompson and his wife, Edith, have three adult children, Gina, Scott, and Karin.

MARK L. WEETER is Associate Vice-President of Academic Affairs and professor in the School of Religion at Oklahoma Wesleyan University, and an ordained elder in The Wesleyan Church. He earned a BT degree from Circleville Bible College (now Ohio Christian University), an M.Div. from Wesley Biblical Seminary, a D.Min. from Reformed Theological Seminary, and a Ph.D. in Theology and Religious Studies from the University of Wales.

Dr. Weeter taught from 1979–1983 at Wesley Bible College; he has been a faculty member at Oklahoma Wesleyan University since 1986. From 1977 until 2006, he also served as either full-time or part-time pastor to a number of congregations. He preaches representing Oklahoma Wesleyan, and is in demand as a camp meeting and revival preacher, having preached in thirty-eight states and four foreign countries. Wipf and Stock published his book, *John Wesley's View and Use of Scripture*, in 2007.

Brenda is Dr. Weeter's wife and partner in ministry. They have three daughters, Allison, Emily, and Megan. The Weeters enjoy traveling.

Other titles in the Wesleyan Theological Perspectives Series!

Passion, Power, and Purpose
Essays on the Art of Contemporary Preaching

Edited by Joseph Coleson

Effective weekly preaching concerns every pastor, both young and old. But even the most seasoned of pastors still questions his effectiveness. "Am I communicating God's words? Am I reaching my congregation? How can I preach more effectively?" Questions like these are hard to find answers to, but *Power, Passion, and Purpose* helps pastors, just like you, become the preacher God intended you to be. Be inspired anew in how and why you preach.

$14.99

"Preaching the Word of God still changes lives and remains a vital task for ministers. Passion, Power, and Purpose will certainly help you enrich your own preaching ministry."

—Dr. Thomas Armiger, General Superintendent,
The Wesleyan Church.

wesleyan
publishing
house

www.wesleyan.org/wph or call toll free
1.800.493.7539 M-F 8 a.m.- 4:30 p.m. EST.

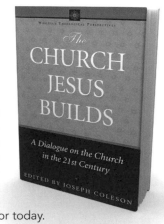

Be Holy

God's Invitation to Understand, Declare, and Experience Holiness

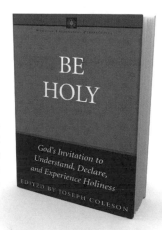

The exhortation "Be Holy, because I am Holy" is a convicting and compelling invitation that has not changed through the centuries. It still conveys the optimism of God's grace available to address both the deepest needs of the human heart and the pressing cultural issues of our day.

$14.99

"For all the confusion these days, holiness is not primarily a doctrine or even an experience, but a life! Thus, as a doctrine it rises or falls on the credibility of the people who profess it. Here are a handful of good, contemporary thinkers who get that. Their wise counsel and practical advice will help move holiness out of the realm of mere theology and into the arena of life. You are in for a treat!"

–Steve DeNeff, Pastor, College Wesleyan Church, Marion, Ind.

wesleyan publishing house

www.wesleyan.org/wph or call toll free

1.800.493.7539 M-F 8 a.m.- 4:30 p.m. EST.

wesleyan
publishing
house

The New Testament Wesleyan Bible Study Commentary Series

An excellent resource for personal study, and especially helpful for those involved in the teaching ministries of the church, The Wesleyan Bible Study Commentaries will encourage and promote life change in believers by applying God's authoritative truth in relevant, practical ways. Written in an easy-to-follow format, you will enjoy studying Scripture insights that are faithful to the Wesleyan-Arminian perspective.

–Steve DeNeff, Pastor, College Wesleyan Church, Marion, Ind.

$269.00

www.wesleyan.org/wph or call toll free

1.800.493.7539 M-F 8 a.m.- 4:30 p.m. EST.

Other titles from Wesleyan Publishing House!

God's Story Revealed:
A Guide for Understanding the Old Testament
Stephen J. Lennox

God's Story Revealed is a concise introduction to the Old Testament that makes God's Word easier to understand for the average reader. Opening chapters give readers the "big picture" of God's plan for His people along with an introduction to the ancient world. Helpful sidebars, key information, and discussion questions are included to enhance readers' understanding.

$19.99

God's Plan Fulfilled:
A Guide for Understanding the New Testament
Kenneth Schenck

God's Plan Fulfilled is a succinct introduction to the New Testament, making God's Word accessible to the average reader by offering background information, an overview of the content, and the tools for understanding key events, ideas, and passages.

$19.99

Making Sense of God's Word:
A Practical Guide for Understanding the Bible
Kenneth Schenck

Making Sense of God's Word offers assistance for the average Christian Bible reader who desires to understand God's Word. Helping the reader sort through the issues of context, genre, and theories of interpretation, Schenck gives practical principles that restore confidence in reading and interpreting Scripture.

$9.99

wesleyan
publishing
house

For more great resources,
go to www.wesleyan.org/wph or call toll free
1.800.493.7539 M-F 8 a.m.- 4:30 p.m. EST.